Oscar de la Renta

Oscar de la Renta

JENNIFER PARK and MOLLY SORKIN, with ANDRÉ LEON TALLEY

Fine Arts Museums of San Francisco

DelMonico Books · Prestel
Munich London New York

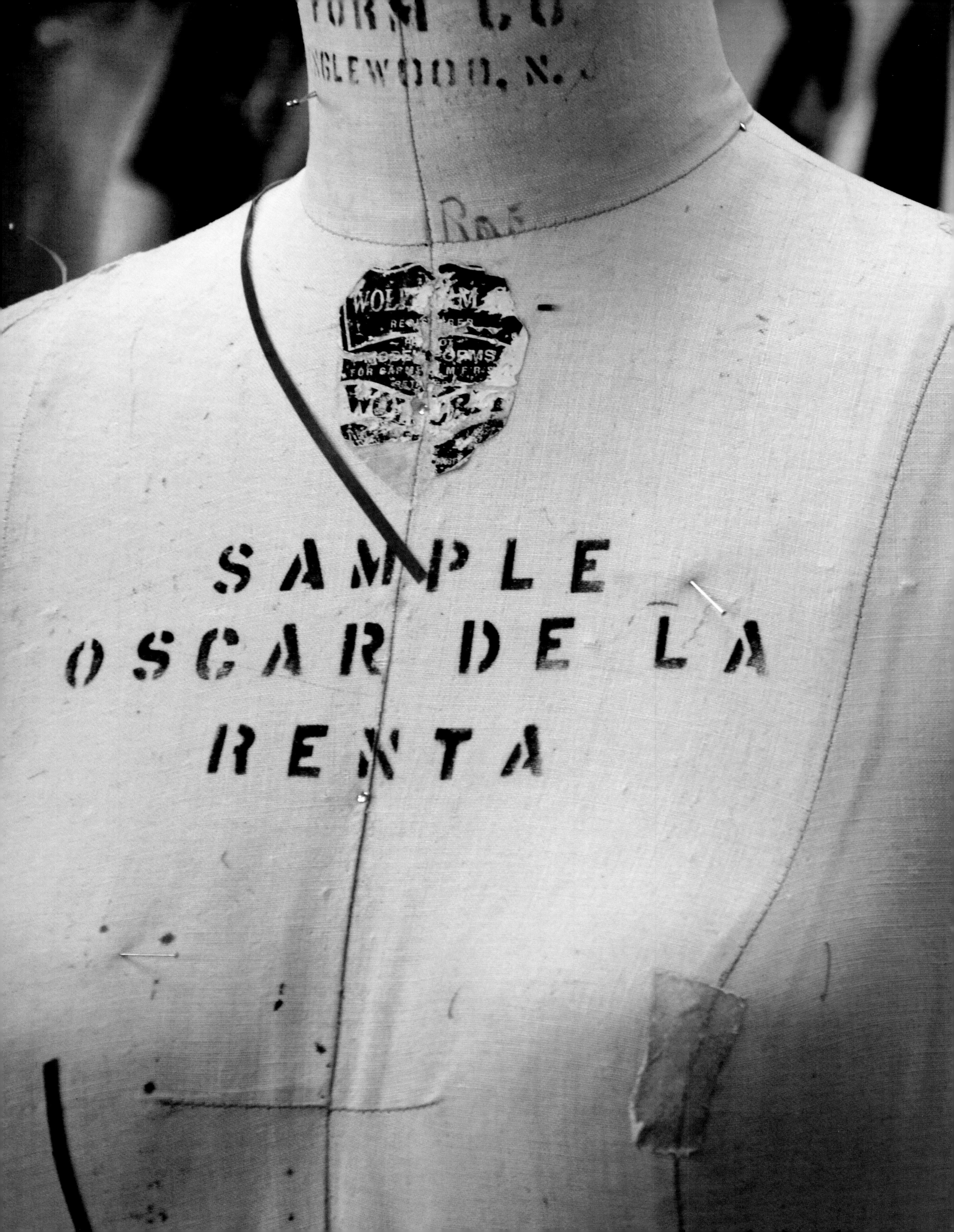
SAMPLE
OSCAR DE LA
RENTA

Contents

(*previous spreads*)
Patrick Demarchelier. Jacquetta Wheeler
wearing an evening dress of black silk tulle.
Originally published in German *Vogue*,
June 2005
Oscar de la Renta workroom, 2015

(*this spread*)
Mario Testino. Sarah Jessica Parker wearing
an evening dress of white silk organza,
fall 2000. Originally published in *Vogue*,
February 2002

(*following spread*)
Inez van Lamsweerde and Vinoodh
Matadin. Oscar de la Renta, 2006

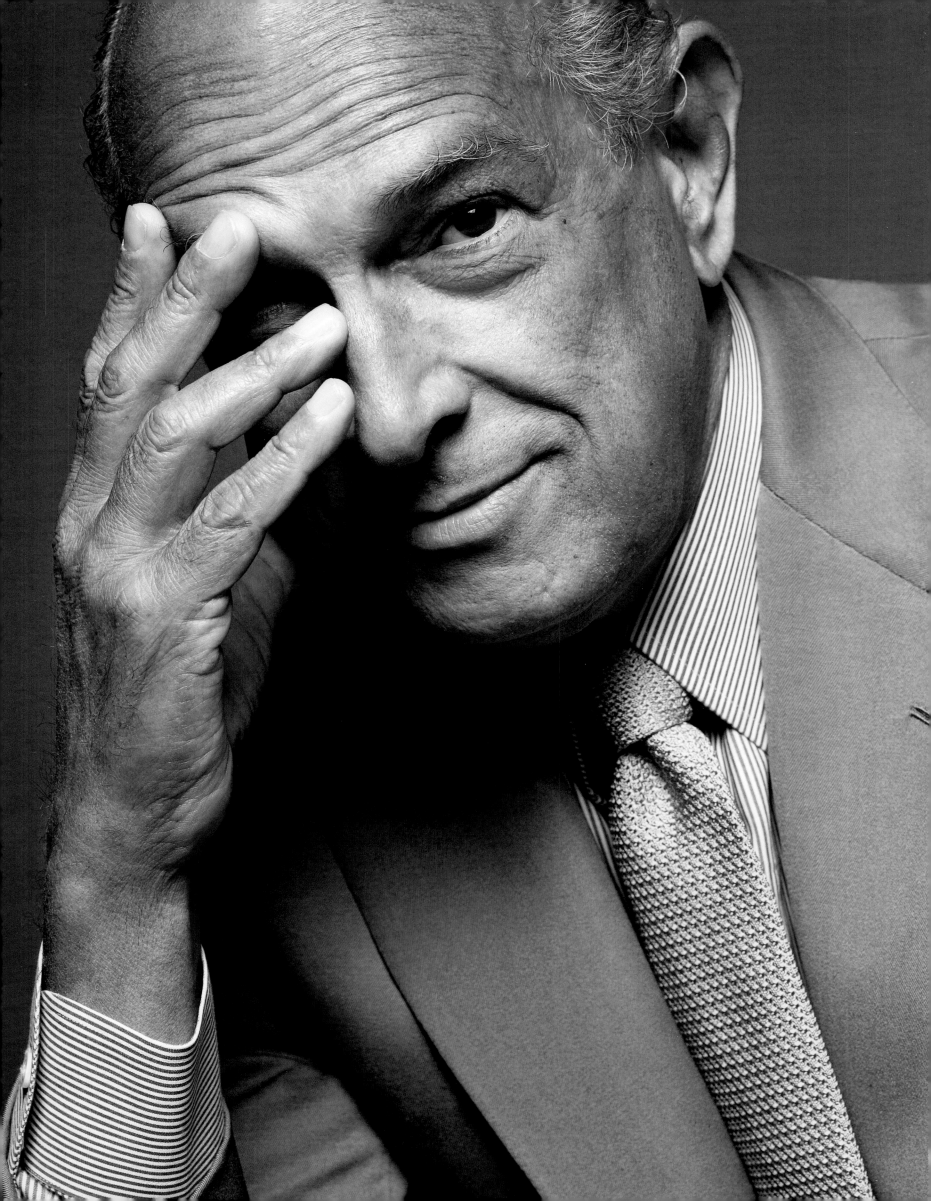

Foreword

RICHARD BENEFIELD

Acting Director of Museums

Fine Arts Museums of San Francisco

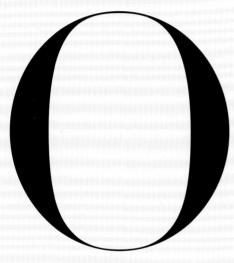

OSCAR DE LA RENTA declared that "fashion is only fashion once a woman puts it on." He celebrated the influential women he dressed by creating designs that reflected the extraordinary personalities of his devoted clients who provided him with inspiration and friendship. He dressed contemporary women, from first ladies to socialites and from Hollywood stars to fashion insiders, in elegant daywear and resplendent evening gowns.

The Fine Arts Museums of San Francisco boast twenty-nine garments by Oscar de la Renta in our costume collection, including an early example of the Queen of Thailand dress (1967) and several couture looks that he created as the lead designer for the couture house Pierre Balmain in Paris. For the opening of the new de Young building in 2005, Oscar de la Renta created a custom gown for the president of our board of trustees, Diane B. Wilsey, which she wore to the inaugural gala. It is especially fitting to host this exhibition in the same building ten years later, and to feature that dress, which was made in a copper-colored silk taffeta to match the metal facade of the de Young.

This presentation was envisioned by Mrs. Wilsey as a tribute to her designer and her friend, and it was brought to fruition by the talented staff at the Museums. The project has been supported further by Oscar de la Renta's widow, Annette de la Renta, and by his family, including Alex and Eliza Bolen. André Leon Talley, lead curator, oversaw the show, with the assistance of Jennifer Park and Molly Sorkin, and all three have contributed important essays to this volume. I further acknowledge the early support of the exhibition, which was provided to us by Mrs. Wilsey, along with Cynthia Fry Gunn and John A. Gunn, presenting sponsors, and The Diana Dollar Knowles Foundation, Marissa Mayer and Zachary Bogue, Paula and Bandel Carano, Stephanie and Jim Marver, Neiman Marcus, Mrs. Carole McNeil, and Mr. and Mrs. Joseph O. Tobin II. Furthermore, I thank our many lenders who have generously shared their works of art with our audiences, adding depth to this groundbreaking exhibition that explores the rich history and extraordinary breadth of Oscar de la Renta's illustrious career.

Acknowledgments

VERY EXHIBITION HAS at least one champion and Diane B. Wilsey, president of the Board of Trustees of the Fine Arts Museums of San Francisco, had the vision and the passion to originate this important retrospective of Oscar de la Renta's work at the de Young. We are grateful to her for her support in so many ways.

This presentation, of course, would not have been possible without the insights, loans, and vital assistance of Oscar's widow, Annette de la Renta, who, among other generosities, graciously allowed a film crew to descend on her beautiful country gardens in Kent, Connecticut, so that we could share the fruits of the de la Rentas' labors with our visitors.

At Oscar de la Renta LLC, I wish to thank chief executive officer, Alex Bolen; executive vice president, Eliza Bolen; creative director, Peter Copping; executive at large, Boaz Mazor; director of administrative services, Doris Amor; former vice president of global communications, Erika Berman; senior vice president of marketing, Michele de Bourbon; vice president of communications, Edith Taichman; archivist, Marianna Sheridan; among many others, all of whom were immensely supportive from the onset of our project, providing access to archival loans, resources, and imagery.

I am grateful to the lead curator of the exhibition, André Leon Talley, whose longtime friendship with Oscar lends a personal note to both the exhibition and the catalogue. He was ably assisted by fashion historians and catalogue essayists, Jennifer Park and Molly Sorkin, who worked closely with Oscar on several exhibitions over the past decade.

For their early support of this exhibition, I express my sincere gratitude to Cynthia Fry Gunn and John A. Gunn, Diane B. Wilsey, The Diana Dollar Knowles Foundation, Marissa Mayer and Zachary Bogue, Paula and Bandel Carano, Stephanie and Jim Marver, Neiman Marcus, Mrs. Carole McNeil, and Mr. and Mrs. Joseph O. Tobin II.

In addition to thanking Mrs. Wilsey, Mrs. de la Renta, and the company for sharing their exquisite pieces by Oscar de la Renta, I thank the following lenders whose important loans enrich the exhibition: Amy Adams; Emmanuel Diemoz at Pierre Balmain, Paris; Barbara Bancroft; Mercedes Bass; Jaqueline Blond; Eliza Bolen; Pamela Bryan; Mrs. Laura Bush and the George W. Bush Presidential Library, Dallas; Petra Slinkard at the Chicago History Museum; Cynthia Amnéus and Adam MacPharlain at the Cincinnati Art Museum; Pat Cleveland; Secretary Hillary Rodham Clinton and the William J. Clinton Presidential Library, Little Rock; Andrew Bolton, Thomas Campbell, and Harold Koda at the Costume Institute at the Metropolitan Museum of Art, New York; Idalia Cruz; Charlene Engelhard; Barbara Bundy and Kevin Jones at the Fashion Institute of Design and Merchandising Museum, Los Angeles; Roberta Garza-Medina; Ann Getty; Jacqueline Hamoui; Jean Druesedow, Joanne Fenn, and Sara Hume at the Kent State University Museum, Ohio; Alexandra Kotur; Princess Marie-Chantal of Greece; Catie Marron; Julia Moore; Fred Dennis, Sonia Dingilian, and Valerie Steele at the Museum at the Fashion Institute of Technology, New York; Sarah Jessica Parker; Dilys Blum and Timothy Rub at the Philadelphia Museum of Art; Amanda Cruz and Dennita Sewell at the Phoenix Art Museum, Arizona; Anita Poll; Kate Irvin and John W. Smith at the Rhode Island School of Design, Providence; Laurie Ann Farrell and Paula Wallace at the Savannah College of Art and Design Museum of Art, Georgia; Jan Shafiroff; Nancy Davis and Margaret Grandine at the Smithsonian Institution, National Museum of American History, Washington, DC; Taylor Swift; Diana Taylor; Myra Walker at the Texas Fashion Collection at the University of North Texas, Denton; Anna Wintour; and Lynn Wyatt.

The sensitive design of the exhibition was executed by Kevin Daly Architects and I am particularly grateful to Kevin Daly and Rachel Lee.

At the Museums, I recognize my colleagues who helped to make this exhibition possible, including: Julian Cox, chief curator and founding curator of photography; Krista Brugnara, director of exhibitions; Jill D'Alessandro, curator of costume and textile arts; Laura Camerlengo, assistant curator of costume and textile arts; Lisa Podos, director of advancement and engagement; Susan Klein, director of marketing and communications; Gary Castro, chief information officer; Sheila Pressley, director of education and public programs; Daniel Meza, chief graphic designer and art director; and Ryan Butterfield, chief preparator. I also acknowledge for their help in this endeavor, Suzy Peterson and Stephen Bowden, executive assistants; Sarah Hammond, exhibitions manager; and Sara Chang, exhibitions coordinator.

This catalogue was gracefully overseen by Leslie Dutcher, director of publications, with assistance from Jane Hyun, editor; Danica Michels Hodge, editor; and Diana K. Murphy, editorial assistant, who helped with the rights and reproductions alongside Jenny Moussa Spring. Kathryn Shedrick managed the copyediting of this volume and Bob Aufuldish created its beautiful design. I thank Mary DelMonico, Karen Farquhar, Ryan Newbanks, and Luke Chase at DelMonico Books | Prestel for their partnership, and I thank Roberto Conti and his colleagues, including Marta Conti, Laura Cuccoli, Ann Faughender, Pietro Petruzzi, and Alfredo Zanatello, at Conti Tipocolor for the impeccable printing of this book. For research support, gratitude is extended to

Lourdes Font at the Fashion Institute of Technology, and to April Calahan and Karen Cannell at FIT's Special Collections and College Archives, Gladys Marcus Library.

I also thank the many artists and photographers who shared their works of art in these pages, including Mert Alas and Marcus Piggott; Neal Barr; Jonathan Becker; Patricia Canino; Claudia Knoepfel and Stefan Indlekofer; Patrick Demarchelier; Arthur Elgort; Robert Fairer; François Halard; Mary Hilliard; Matti Hillig; Annie Leibovitz; Danielle Levitt; Peter Lindbergh; Craig McDean; Steven Meisel; Sheila Metzner; James Nord; Gladys Perint Palmer; Denis Piel; David Sims; Lea Suzuki; Kevin Tachman; Mario Testino; Inez van Lamsweerde and Vinoodh Matadin; Ellen von Unwerth; Bruce Weber; and Miguel Yatco. Thanks is also given to the studios, estates, and archives that assisted in preparing the imagery for our book, including Brandon Eng at Art + Commerce; Stefanie Breslin at Art Partner Licensing; Elizabeth Covintree at the Arthur Elgort Studio; Hannah Hayden at Assouline; Theresa Dellegrazie at August Image; Marianne Brown, Gretchen Fenston, Lindsay Foster, Deanna Scopino, Kyle Tannler, and Shawn Waldron at Condé Nast Licensing and Archives; Joe Maloney at Corbis; Vanessa Fairer at the Robert Fairer studio; the Estate of Helmut Newton; Jina Park and Lisa Lebowitz at the Fairchild Archives; Foto di Matti; Catherine Gachet at Galliera Roger-Violett; Jodie Steck at the George W. Bush Presidential Library; Sarah Zimmer at Getty Images; Maryn Rich at the Irving Penn Foundation; Jesse Blatt at the J. Blatt Agency; Daniel Paik at the Jonathan Becker Studio; Paula Wegner at Neal Barr Photography; the *New York Times* archive; Marianna Sheridan and Nadine Lorioth at the Oscar de la Renta Archive; Thierry-Maxime Loriot at Studio Peter Lindbergh; Rosemary Marrow at Redux Pictures; Erin Harris at the Richard Avedon Foundation; Billy Vong at Trunk Archive; Herbert Ragan at the William J. Clinton Presidential Library; and Kate Johnson at Wolf Literary Services.

RICHARD BENEFIELD
Acting Director of Museums
Fine Arts Museums of San Francisco

Sunlit Memories of Oscar

"There is light within a person of light, and it lights up the whole universe."
—from the Gospel according to Thomas

**OD, DO I MISS OSCAR!** I miss the warmth of those other suns that accompanied him everywhere he went: to work, on vacations, at dinner, and in his three beautiful homes, in Kent, Connecticut, in his native Dominican Republic, and in his pied-à-terre on Park Avenue in New York. Oscar carried with him the warmth of paradise, surely drawn from the sheer happiness of his childhood, growing up in a tropical environment in a huge family, surrounded by love. Throughout his life, there was always love and laughter and it infused everything he took to task, be it the designing of a simple cashmere coat, a suit, or a gorgeous evening dress; preparing a lovely dinner party; or tending to his gardens. Oscar loved life, and the light from within him beamed out to his world.

During a Saturday blizzard in New York, as Oscar was in the last moments of finalizing one of his collections, one could feel the sun's warmth radiating from him. When he entered a room, he filled it with his own personal joy. Often, in his rich soothing voice, he would greet me, calling out "Talleyrand," after the famous French diplomat. It made me stand up straight, taller in my shoes.

One always tried to live up to Oscar's standards. He had the most impeccable manners, like a person from another era who carried such admirable qualities as courtesy, respect, and kind gestures toward others. He presented his best foot forward always, as part of a code of living. Even in swimming trunks or jeans, Oscar looked handsome, elegant, turned out, fit, and possessed of inner strength from a light unknown.

• • •

I met Oscar de la Renta in 1974, when I first arrived in New York from Brown University, where I had been studying for an advanced degree in French Literature. Diana Vreeland introduced us, as she was one of the best friends of Oscar (see fig. 35) and his first wife, Françoise de Langlade, the former editor in chief of Paris *Vogue*.

Mrs. Vreeland arranged my first official job at Andy Warhol's *Interview* magazine, and after six months, I was hired as an editor at John Fairchild's *Women's Wear*

Daily. Prior to these positions, I had volunteered at the Metropolitan Museum of Art's Costume Institute. Oscar and Françoise invited me to their table at the Gala in December 1975, and, soon after, to dinner at their home, which is now the apartment of Valentino when he is in Manhattan. When I moved to Paris to become the bureau chief of *Women's Wear Daily* and *W*, I would return to the States in August, and the de la Rentas would invite me down to their home in the Dominican Republic.

From one career trajectory to the other, Oscar remained a loyal friend. Our lives were as intertwined as stitching. We both spoke the same language of fashion. Throughout his life, Oscar's main motivation in his work was to create a signature style that did not detract from, but enhanced, the natural beauty and grace of the individual wearing his designs. He understood the elegance of simplicity, and at the same time, the necessity of opulence, the baroque, and the romantic notion of beautiful evening clothes.

I can remember all of the great moments and the fabulous ensembles Oscar designed over the course of more than four decades. My memory for clothes is, if I say so myself, exceptional. I never take notes at fashion shows, and I can today remember clothes I saw nearly a half century ago. I can summon up Oscar's gowns inspired by Marcel Proust's masterpiece *Remembrance of Things Past*, which were worn by his wife Annette de la Renta and Nan Kempner, two of the most elegant American patrons of Parisian haute couture in contemporary memory.

• • •

Diana Vreeland, both a mentor and a friend, and the great editor John Fairchild were my finest teachers. Mrs. Vreeland taught me how to look at beautiful clothes from within to without; in other words, to see that the interior construction and linings were as essential and meticulously considered as the exterior fabric and embellishments. Mr. Fairchild taught me how to write about clothes and investigate the choices that were made by the person wearing them or designing them. This knowledge, of course, informed the ways that I looked at Oscar's works of art.

The first spring after I moved to Paris, Mrs. Vreeland penned me a letter that I have kept to this day, and I repeat it here in its original format:

> April 25, 1978
> André,
> I want to tell you that I think your report on the Saint Laurent collection is one of the best pieces of writing on fashion I have ever read.
> I talked with Yves about it yesterday and we both agree that it is a masterpiece of description.
> All of your pieces—Valentino, Lagerfeld, Lulu's party, etc.—are all very remarkable. Everything is so immediate, gay, and totally clear!
> Mr. André Leon Talley
> Women's Wear Daily
> 39 rue Cambon
> Paris
> France

I keep a copy of this letter close to me, inside of a book jacket. The original letter, one of the most important keepsakes of my life, is safely tucked away in my grandmother's handkerchief drawer in her bedroom in her house in Durham, North Carolina. This was where I grew up and first learned about high style from my grandmother and her siblings, my aunts, my cousins, and all the fantastic black women in our family church. It was on Sundays that style turned out: the best hats, gloves, polished shoes, and handbags. It was when we as a family, part of a bigger history and culture, put on our "Sunday best." It was surely this groundwork that prepared me to understand and write about Oscar's exquisite creations.

John Richardson, the great Picasso expert, once told me that he and Diana Vreeland had a long conversation about my dispatches from Paris in *Women's Wear Daily*. "Diana thinks you describe clothes as if you had actually worn the dresses yourself," he said.

• • •

One day in January 2001, Mica Ertegun, a member of the Best-Dressed Hall of Fame, had lunch with me in the Condé Nast cafeteria designed by Frank Gehry. To celebrate her fortieth wedding anniversary in the coming April to the record and music titan Ahmet Ertegun, Mica, who has been dressed by Madame Grès, Christian Dior, and Pierre Balmain, told me that she had to have something special from Oscar for the occasion's ball.

Ahmet had given his loving wife a ruby collar from the legendary house of JAR, Paris, and Mica wanted her look to complement the necklace. Off we went to see Oscar, and he came up with the idea of a sapphire-blue shirt and a ruffled geranium-red skirt, a combination that was repeated over and over again in his collections after that, for many other clients. The skirt and shirt displayed in the de Young's exhibition is one of my favorite examples to establish the remarkable Oscar style: a special order for a distinguished customer who wanted the ease and practicality of a silk blouse and a dinner skirt. He understood Mica's personal style, and he embellished it with flourishes of papery silk ruffles and bold color (see figs. 2–4).

At that same party, held on the roof of the Saint Regis hotel in New York, Oscar's wife Annette opted for her husband's black velvet dress with diamante shoulder straps and bows (see fig. 5 and pl. 23), inspired by John Singer Sargent's famous painting *Madame X (Madame Pierre Gautreau)* (1883–1884, The Metropolitan Museum of Art, New York). Both Mica and Annette stood out at the occasion, each reflecting their own Oscar style.

• • •

Some of Oscar de la Renta's best work was produced in the decade when he designed the haute couture collections, twice a year, for the Paris house, Pierre Balmain. His clients and friends loved those collections and many examples are featured in this exhibition. The black velvet dress worn by his wife Annette to the Ertegun ball is just one beautiful example of his many creations that were embellished with extravagant details.

Often in Paris, Oscar and I would have long conversations, and his knowledge of literature, art, music, and social history was amazing. He could literally talk about almost anything. At one point, a discussion turned to the inspiration for one of the most important female Proustian characters: Oriane, Duchesse de Guermantes. I showed him a photo of the model for that famous character, the Comtesse Élisabeth de Greffulhe (see fig. 6). She was captured by the famous photographer Nadar, in a black and white dress by Charles Frederick Worth, the famous English-born couturier who made his name in Paris. Oscar transformed that image into a beautiful black-and-white ball gown for the autumn/winter 1999–2000 collection (pls. 69–70).

Comtesse de Greffulhe was recognized as the best-dressed hostess of the most important social salon in Belle Époque Paris. In his story, Proust makes exquisite descriptions of Oriane's wardrobe at every turn. Every detail is narrated to convey the importance of the Duchesse and her impact on society through her elegance, her wit—and her clothes.

Annette de la Renta, also one of the world's best-dressed and most elegant women, served a role in Oscar's life that is without parallel. Along with attending society balls and dinners, she is on the board of the Metropolitan Museum of Art as well as the boards of the Morgan Library and Museum, the New York Public Library, the Rockefeller University, and the Animal Medical Center. Annette was the Oriane of Oscar's private existence and his professional world. She was not only the love of his life but his muse.

When Oscar was really happy with a piece, he would often say: "My wife would look wonderful in this dress." Or: "Will Annette wear it?"

So many of Annette's clothes are of dazzling beauty. Some suggest references to Spain (see pls. 12–26), from the drama of one of Francisco de Goya's paintings of the Duchess of Alba, to one of Diego Velázquez's Infantas. Yet at home, especially in Kent, Connecticut, on a Saturday morning, in the early summer, Annette may be found in a simple button-front shirt with the sleeves rolled up, jeans, high platform espadrilles, and an old Saint Laurent panama hat, spiked with a gold-leaf metal pin.

• • •

It is at Brook Hill Farm, where the de la Rentas lived when they were not in the Dominican Republic, that one can experience the true wonder and the sunny happiness of Oscar's life, which was lived in gardens (see figs. 7–10). So many inspirations from his gardens bloom on the surfaces of his ball gowns, seasonal day clothes, and embroideries (see pls. 54–66).

"What a perfect May morning this is, one where I imagine he would have risen before us, fixed his coffee, and gone out into his garden. He would have stood upon his mount and watered the rows, sorting his head for the day," writes the poet, professor, and author Elizabeth Alexander, who wrote "Praise Song for the Day" for President Obama's 2009 inauguration. This extract, about her relationship to her husband of fifteen years, before his death, is from her memoir *The Light of the World*, which is one of my favorite books.

Oscar had so many perfect mornings at Brook Hill Farm. The gardens that he was so passionate about and proud of have the grandeur of those of English estates or of many wonderful and elegant allées on the grounds of the Pavlovsk Palace, in Saint

7 Oscar de la Renta in his gardens at Brook Hill Farm in Kent, Connecticut
8–9 Oscar de la Renta's gardens at Brook Hill Farm in Kent, Connecticut

Petersburg, Russia. Noble yet simple odes to nature, Oscar's gardens symbolize the beauty of a life fulfilled in achievement and cultivation.

Oscar had loved nature since his childhood, but he never dreamed that he would one day have his own garden. He spent nearly four decades creating his gardens, starting with advice from the English landscape architect Sir Russell Page. In a book that Oscar published on the Internet one weekend with the help of his staff and his gardener, Oscar wrote: "A garden is the most spiritual and pure of joys that one is ever likely to encounter. It's a communion with nature and beauty in the most simple and fundamental form, to be appreciated and understood is an experience that should be lived at every instant. It also teaches you patience and humility." Oscar's gardens are not only beautiful, but they are living testaments of his grace, enlivened by his sun.

(opposite)
10 François Halard. Oscar and Annette de la Renta at their home in Kent, Connecticut, 2008

(following spread)
11 Steven Meisel. Amber Valletta wearing a cocktail dress of silk jacquard. Originally published in *Vogue*, June 2006

MOLLY SORKIN

Oscar de la Renta

N NOVEMBER 3, 2014, a veritable who's who of the worlds of fashion, society, politics, and the arts gathered at the Church of Saint Ignatius Loyola in New York City to mourn the passing of designer Oscar de la Renta (1932–2014), who recently had died from cancer.[1] Cardinal Theodore McCarrick presided over the formal requiem mass—a fittingly distinguished memorial for de la Renta, who made an indelible mark on the city where he launched his American career more than fifty years earlier. The church's ornate interior was filled with an extravagant display of lush greenery that evoked the designer's beloved gardens at his home in Kent, Connecticut. From high in the choir loft came the voice of tenor Vittorio Grigolo, whose emotive singing enhanced the solemn beauty of the occasion. The designer's close friends gave the readings: former secretaries of state Henry Kissinger and Hillary Rodham Clinton; former New York mayor Michael Bloomberg; and the editor in chief of *Vogue*, Anna Wintour. Among the hundreds of close family members, friends, and colleagues who came to pay their respects were the designers Valentino Garavani, Donna Karan, Ralph Lauren, and Diane von Furstenberg; media moguls Rupert Murdoch and Barry Diller; and devoted clients such as philanthropist Mercedes Bass, broadcasting legend Barbara Walters, and former First Lady Laura Bush. Paparazzi, confined to the meridian on Park Avenue, captured the scene as guests departed into the bright fall day to the exuberant melody of Beethoven's "Ode to Joy."

Óscar Arístides Ortiz Renta Fiallo was born on July 22, 1932, in Santo Domingo, Dominican Republic, the youngest and the only son in a family of seven children.[2] Although far removed from the fashion capitals he would later dominate, de la Renta's early life was filled with the vivid sights, sounds, and fragrant smells that were the earliest building blocks of what would become his signature style. Much later in life de la Renta recounted to fashion critic Sarah Mower the "colors, flowers, sunshine" of his native country and the "white ruffles and flounces" worn by his grandmother.[3] He also recalled the beautiful Russian mistress of his uncle, who would regale him with "incredible, magical stories about Russia and traveling through Europe, stories that fed my imagination and made me dream."[4]

Though de la Renta grew up in an impoverished Catholic country ruled by a military dictatorship, his mother's family was well connected, both socially and politically, and his father, originally from Puerto Rico, had a successful insurance business that he hoped his only son would take over someday.[5] But de la Renta's interests lay in the arts, and from a young age his artistic talent was encouraged, initially by a local priest, and later by his mother, who gave the approval for him to go to the local art school at the age of fourteen.[6] De la Renta remembered this formative period of his life: "I'd go to high school from eight to one, and then to art school from two till seven in the evening. I was really lucky, because the school was at its height then. Because of the Spanish Civil War, when so many creative people had had to emigrate, we had extraordinary teachers: José Gausachs [Josep Gausachs Armengol], José Vela Zanetti, Domingo Pascual."[7]

Upon his high school graduation in 1950, de la Renta hoped to go to Spain to continue his education at the Real Academia de Bellas Artes de San Fernando in Madrid, where his friend Fernando Peña Defilló (b. 1928), who would become one of the Dominican Republic's most celebrated artists, was attending school.[8] De la Renta left for Spain in 1951, and enrolled in the Academia to study painting.[9]

Oscar de la Renta spent almost ten years in Spain, and it was there that he made the tentative transition from aspiring artist to fashion designer and immersed himself in Spanish culture.[10] He later wrote, "The sights, sounds, and drama of Spanish culture—bullfights, flamenco, and the most festive celebrations, such as the traditional *ferias* of Seville and Jerez and *fallas* of Valencia, were burned forever in my imagination, defining my own aesthetic."[11]

On his first night in Madrid, de la Renta went to see the acclaimed flamenco dancer Pilar López, an experience he described to Mower as "an unbelievable revelation."[12] He also wrote, "I fell madly for Spain, its people, its landscape, and life in Madrid."[13] After his first year of art school, he embarked on a trip around southern Spain that would dramatically influence his future work as a designer (see fig 13): "I was traveling third class with all the peasants who were on their way to the olive harvest, and there was a whole gypsy family of about thirty or forty people on board. I ended up being invited to a gypsy wedding, which went on for three days, and being mesmerized by the sight of all the women wearing flamenco dresses in extraordinary colors."[14]

De la Renta was equally captivated by what he saw in Madrid, and his life there became less about school and more about the city's late-night socializing.[15] The designer recounted how his father encouraged him to return home to enter the family business, but he decided to stay. Without his father's support he needed to earn money, so he "started doing fashion sketches for newspapers, magazines, and fashion houses"—his first foray into the world of fashion.[16]

Among de la Renta's circle of acquaintances in Madrid were the former fashion designer and all-around Renaissance woman Ana de Pombo and her husband, interior decorator Pablo Oliveras.[17] De Pombo had worked in Paris as the designer for Jeanne

Paquin, and her assistant had once been Antonio del Castillo, de la Renta's future employer.[18] De Pombo and Oliveras were also friends with the legendary Spanish couturier Cristóbal Balenciaga. Through this group of friends de la Renta obtained an entry-level position at EISA, the Madrid location of Balenciaga's couture house.[19] For de la Renta it proved to be an important training ground. He explained, "I'd never been to fashion school, I was an art student, so thus far my sketches were all illustrations, not working drawings. So all of a sudden I had this amazing advantage. I could go into the sample rooms, look at the clothes, see how they were cut and made, touch the fabric, and learn about it. Then I could understand properly where to place the dart and the flounce."[20] His job, as he described it, was to "sketch dresses to send to customers with a fabric sample, or several samples in different colors, attached to the drawing."[21] Although he was not yet designing, de la Renta was exposed through this repetitive work to Balenciaga's technical expertise and immense creativity, an education in and of itself. In explaining the low level of his position, de la Renta told fashion industry leader Fern Mallis in an interview, "I was picking pins from the floor."[22]

One of de la Renta's earliest creations was the debutante dress he designed in 1956 for Beatrice Cabot Lodge, the daughter of American ambassador to Spain John Davis Lodge, who made her debut in Madrid.[23] The story was featured in *Life* magazine, with the smiling debutante on the cover wearing a festive Spanish cape decorated with colorful ribbons and rosettes.[24] The magazine declared, "The most serenaded, most admired, most applauded young lady in all Spain was an American."[25]

The accompanying photo-essay chronicled her coming-out party and the week leading up to it, with several photographs of Lodge in her debutante dress. In one of the images, the nascent designer is seen adjusting the skirt of the ball gown during a fitting (fig. 14). In de la Renta's own account of how he came to design the "white tulle double-tiered bubble dress," he sheds light on the way that social relationships would become so integral to his career: "A dress I had designed for a friend, and had made up by my tailor, caught the eye of his [Lodge's] wife, Francesca. . . . After I made a dress for Francesca, she asked me if I would make a dress for her daughter Beatrice for her coming-out party at the American Embassy in Madrid."[26]

Although de la Renta and his design were uncredited in the *Life* article, he had still landed his first appearance in a major American magazine despite not yet being a full-fledged fashion designer and having no real connection to the United States other than Lodge and her family.[27] Like the young American who wore his dress, de la Renta had also made a debut of sorts, and it foreshadowed the strong relationships he would develop with his American clients and the magazines that would feature his work for years to come. For de la Renta's first major commission, he was in essence working for himself, an auspicious beginning for someone whose name would become forever linked with American fashion.

By 1959 de la Renta had grown "restless" in Madrid and wanted to move to Paris, where he believed he would have more opportunities.[28] Based on his much-improved portfolio of sketches, he was offered a position at Christian Dior. But on the suggestion

14 Oscar de la Renta fitting Beatrice Cabot Lodge's debutante dress in Madrid, June 1, 1956. Originally published in *Life*, July 9, 1956

of "Jorge Granados, a painter friend from Madrid who was now living in Paris," de la Renta also approached Granados's friend, the Spanish couturier Antonio del Castillo, who was the designer at the storied French couture house of Jeanne Lanvin, which had been renamed Lanvin-Castillo during his tenure.[29] The prospect of being an assistant to a Spanish-speaking designer for more money than he would make at Dior was too good to pass up, so de la Renta took the job at Lanvin instead. The increased responsibility of this new position required more skill than he had at the time, so he returned to Madrid to prepare for his move, and, most importantly, immersed himself in a crash course in fashion draping, where he implored his instructor to "teach me everything she knew in the space of two weeks."[30]

It was at Lanvin-Castillo that de la Renta officially became a fashion designer in his own right. Although working under someone else's name, he and fellow assistant Dominic Toubeix were able to see their creations come to life.[31] In 1962 de la Renta designed an ice-blue silk cocktail ensemble that consisted of a fitted sheath dress and swing coat that was covered in blue ostrich feathers (fig. 15) that would have trembled as the wearer moved, creating an ethereal effect.[32] Christened "The Blue Angel," it appeared in the March 1962 issues of both French and American *Vogue*, photographed by William Klein.[33] It is the earliest known piece designed by de la Renta to appear in any fashion publication. A month prior, an illustration of the same coat appeared on the front page of *Women's Wear Daily*, worn by Princesse Ghislaine de Polignac, who was described by the publication as "one of the smartest women in Paris."[34]

The use of feathers as a decorative element is a device that de la Renta would return to again and again. For his spring 1992 collection, he designed updated versions of the Lanvin-Castillo piece, this time in hot Caribbean pink and bright sunset orange. These shorter, flirtier ensembles were worn on the runway by models-of-the-moment Linda Evangelista and Naomi Campbell, who personified the joyful exuberance of de la Renta's designs. In 1999, then as the designer for the couture house Pierre Balmain, de la Renta once again revisited "The Blue Angel," this time reimaging the ensemble as a feathered, strapless jumpsuit with a regal, floor-sweeping evening coat. The effect was both playful and elegant, like de la Renta himself.

De la Renta remained at Lanvin-Castillo for three years, embracing life in the French capital and finessing his craft at a couture house that had been in operation since the turn of the twentieth century. His arrival in Paris coincided with a pivotal time in fashion, when the long-standing tradition of couture clothing—made to measure using the finest quality materials—was on the brink of being usurped by ready-to-wear clothing, its mass-produced and less expensive counterpart.

In November 1962, a small news item appeared on the front page of *Women's Wear Daily* announcing a "New Man in Town."[35] It went on to report, "There's a new Paris designer in New York talking about new assignments and he could move into the big league. . . . His name—Oscar Renta, assistant to Castillo."[36] De la Renta was passing through New York on his way to the Dominican Republic for Christmas. He was also keeping his eyes and ears open to employment prospects and had brought along a portfolio of sketches that he had been working on for a month.[37] This intentional detour

15 William Klein. Evening ensemble of a dress of pale-blue silk and coat of pale-blue silk and ostrich feathers, Lanvin-Castillo. Originally published in *Vogue*, March 15, 1962

was ostensibly motivated by an interest in working as a ready-to-wear designer in the industry's undisputed mecca.

While in New York, de la Renta's friend Count Lanfranco Rasponi, who managed public relations for Elizabeth Arden, arranged for him to be seated next to the cosmetics mogul (who also had a successful custom clothing business) at the Spoleto Festival of Two Worlds Ball being held at the Plaza Hotel.[38] It was a savvy move, as Rasponi knew that Arden had been without a permanent designer for her line of custom clothing since 1959.[39] De la Renta also would have been very aware of Arden, as his current employer, Antonio Castillo, had been her designer from 1945 to 1950.

Rasponi's seating arrangements were a success: Arden was intrigued that de la Renta was the protégé of her former designer, Castillo.[40] In de la Renta, she recognized a charming, talented Paris-trained couturier with an impeccable, although short, employment pedigree. She also realized that having him as her in-house designer might raise the profile of her establishment. After seeing his sketches, Arden was ready to hire de la Renta immediately, but Christian Dior New York also had offered him a job as a ready-to-wear designer.[41]

De la Renta considered his options very carefully and consulted Diana Vreeland, the editor in chief of *Vogue*, to whom he had been given a letter of introduction.[42] According to de la Renta, her sage advice was to take the job with Arden because even though he saw his future in ready-to-wear fashion, at Dior he would be "working behind a very big name, and it will be very difficult to make a name for yourself."[43]

Two months later *Women's Wear Daily* reported: "PARIS IMPORT: Jetting in from the Continent on Wednesday . . . Oscar de la Renta, formerly with Lanvin-Castillo . . . he is joining Elizabeth Arden to design the custom collection . . . the first one for spring" (see fig. 16).[44] De la Renta's reasons for leaving Lanvin-Castillo were probably more complex than just his desire to enter the burgeoning ready-to-wear market. In his interview with Mower, he told the story of how an illustration for one of his daywear designs for Lanvin-Castillo was requested by *Women's Wear Daily* for the cover: "I was so proud that I'd designed that coat, though I didn't expect any credit for it. I'll never forget: as I handed him [Castillo] the sketch, he looked me in the eye and said, 'I knew that when I designed this coat, it was going to be great.' I was stunned."[45] Toubeix, his fellow assistant, reminded him, "You're working for him—it's his coat."[46] De la Renta had ambition and wanted to make a name for himself, which he realized he could never do under Castillo.

De la Renta's departure a month before the spring collection was to be shown coincided with a turbulent time at Lanvin-Castillo. A week after *Women's Wear Daily* broadcast de la Renta's hiring at Arden, it broke a series of reports about Castillo's departure from his own firm. On January 9 it announced that "Castillo is ready to resign from Lanvin."[47] One day later they reported that Castillo was ill, but that he would "present the collection if he has to be carried to the studio on a stretcher."[48] The next day the paper reported that his design duties were being temporarily passed to a milliner who had previously worked for Pierre Cardin.[49] Castillo's remaining assistant, Toubeix, was reportedly "suffering a nervous depression" due to "worry over Castillo's health and the strain of making the new collection."[50] This manifested itself in Toubeix's arrest for "throwing a rock through the Lanvin window," resulting in his termination.[51] De la Renta's absence during this time was surely felt. Later he reminisced, noting the irony that if he had stayed at Lanvin, he probably would have ended up as the designer.[52]

Oscar de la Renta presented his first collection for Elizabeth Arden on March 7, 1963. *Women's Wear Daily* ran a preview of the collection two weeks before, noting that he designed it on "that famous ex-Castillo mannequin, that sunny gazelle, Diane."[53] Coats were noted for their "sophistication," and "ultra pretty evening gowns" were highlighted.[54] Accompanying the article was a photograph of de la Renta reclining on a couch in his office looking relaxed and confident (fig. 17).

De la Renta's fall collection, his second for Elizabeth Arden, earned him his first review by the *New York Times*, which praised the clothes for their "strong contemporary look" (fig. 61).[55] In the article de la Renta stated, "I design clothes for women to wear. I am not interested in shock tactics. . . . I just want to make beautiful clothes."[56] He would make similar statements throughout his career, always emphasizing that his driving motivation was to make the women he dressed feel and look their most beautiful. His collection demonstrated a painter's understanding of color and favored the strong Spanish hues of a bullfighter's cape, with evening garments in bright fuchsia (see pl. 13) and "hot yellow."[57] Both colors would become trademarks of the designer. Happy Rockefeller, the new bride of the governor of New York, purchased a number of de la Renta's custom pieces from this collection for her honeymoon in Europe (fig. 19).[58]

Although essentially still a couturier, de la Renta created custom designs that were also available in ready-to-wear versions, which were sold in the Arden salons.[59] It was this fast-growing and profitable sector of the industry that drew him to New York in the first place and that younger women, especially, were embracing. The *New York Times* pointed out that in addition to drawing New York's established tastemakers, his fashion shows attracted young attendees, "many of whom were not long past their teens."[60]

De la Renta was favorably compared to Balenciaga in that he relied "on cut rather than detail for his effects."[61] In de la Renta's hands a simple day coat in a bold plaid was both jaunty and elegant (fig. 18). By his third collection, the *New York Times* identified what was to become a hallmark of de la Renta's style: "His austerity in day clothes is balanced by extravagance for evening, including masses of ruffles, and that how-low-can-you-go neckline that no collection can be without."[62]

In 1964 *Women's Wear Daily* reported on a rumor that de la Renta was headed back to Paris to open a "couture operation in [Arden's] Paris salon" and that "RTW [ready-to-wear] copies would be made in Paris, then shipped to New York."[63] The intriguing rumor proved to be false but would play into de la Renta's eventual departure from the company. De la Renta continued working for Arden in New York until 1965, when his final collection, for the spring/summer season, was shown in February.[64] Among the designs was an evening ensemble that appeared in *Vogue*, April 1, 1965, hinted at two major themes present throughout de la Renta's career—a garden influence was

(opposite)

17 Oscar de la Renta being interviewed in his office at Elizabeth Arden, February 20, 1963. Originally published in *Women's Wear Daily*, February 25, 1963

(following spread)

18 House photograph of plaid wool day coat, Elizabeth Arden by Oscar de la Renta, autumn/winter 1963

19 House photograph of an evening dress of gold and pink silk damask, Elizabeth Arden by Oscar de la Renta, autumn/winter 1963

evident in the large painterly floral fabric, and the matching shawl with small ruffle had a touch of Spanish flair.

De la Renta's decision to leave Elizabeth Arden was directly related to his long-standing interest in working in ready-to-wear fashion. In the Mallis interview he explained how he "tried to convince her [Arden] that she should go into the ready-to-wear business, and at first she agreed."[65] He met with Ben Shaw, who owned several Seventh Avenue labels, including Jane Derby. The label's designer was about to retire from her eponymous line, and de la Renta and Shaw planned to retire the Jane Derby name as well and fold the label into Elizabeth Arden, giving Arden a dedicated ready-to-wear division. In the end, Arden shied away from the venture, and de la Renta took the opportunity to leave Elizabeth Arden and partner with Shaw as the designer for Jane Derby.[66] De la Renta ensured that his name would be on the label, giving himself top billing: "Oscar de la Renta for Jane Derby."[67] Derby died soon after de la Renta's first collection in 1965, and the company's name was soon changed to Oscar de la Renta.[68]

De la Renta's success as a ready-to-wear designer was immediate. He brought invaluable experience working at the highest levels of fashion and a heightened aesthetic enhanced by his artistic training and years of living in Europe. The *New York Times* declared his first collection, for fall 1965, to be "a triumph."[69] It singled out his evening clothes, noting that, "the real excitement began with the long evening dresses."[70] A standout from the collection was a slim celadon evening gown with a standaway neckline and long sleeves. Ornate embellishment on the bodice and cuffs created a trompe l'oeil jewelry effect, the only decoration on the otherwise austere design.

In 1967 de la Renta won his first "Winnie," the Coty Award for womenswear, at the American Fashion Critics' Awards, the fashion industry's equivalent to the Academy Awards (see fig. 20).[71] In her foreword for the ceremony's program, jury chairman Patricia Peterson, the fashion editor for the *New York Times*, wrote: "Mr. de la Renta is hailed for his 'outstanding contribution to fashion'—clothes that are elegant and expensive; haute couture made plausible in ready-to-wear. Mr. de la Renta's designs are dramatic in this sharp contemporary world and will be worn with a flourish by his many socialite customers."[72]

De la Renta won the award for his fall 1967 line, which he called "The Road of Spices," a richly textured collection layered with multiethnic Eastern influences.[73] A script for the award presentation describes the visual splendor of the clothes: "The allure of the Tartar coats, thickly bordered in fur, of Cossack tunics and the marvelous bold capes of Afghanistan, of heavily jeweled ceremonial robes and kaftans, Mongolian sashes and Turkish harem belts, Scheherazadian clothes in rich fabrics, jewel-colored, spice-colored, in sumptuous Persian brocades, velvets, and laces showered with fabulous baubles and beads" (pl. 2).[74]

As a counterpoint to the opulence, the collection included a very modern grouping of sleek column dresses, both long and short, in bold colors and subtly shimmering brocades, each with a single circular cutout detail, and most with asymmetric necklines (see pl. 6). During the fashion show, models walked to the exotic melody of Rimsky-Korsakov's "Song of India" to complete the sensuous mood that de la Renta was

20 Oscar de la Renta with models wearing designs from his fall 1967 collection, for which he won his first Coty Award. Originally published in the *New York Times*, September 29, 1967

evoking.[75] Fashion critic Eugenia Sheppard summed up the entire effect: "Soft, silky and jeweled, the collection was like opium to any woman who craves sheer beauty in her clothes."[76]

The following year de la Renta won his second Winnie.[77] In her review of his fall 1968 collection, which once again looked eastward, Sheppard wrote that he had "produced more sheer, undiluted, and certainly, lavish beauty than I have ever seen all at once in a Seventh Avenue or even Paris collection."[78] For de la Renta, a luxurious printed metallic lamé evening dress with gold ornamentation and sable trim represented the true spirit of the collection (pls. 48–49).[79] A black and white "Le Smoking," or tuxedo-style, cocktail dress with a plunging neckline also featured gold embellishment, almost like jewelry (pl. 1). He favored trouser ensembles as well—long tunics paired with pants (see pl. 34)—especially to wear at night. Glamorous evening pajamas would become a staple of de la Renta's style, symbolizing the type of relaxed opulence that appealed to his sophisticated clientele.

De la Renta's fashion shows attracted the highest tier of international society, and this one was no exception. In attendance for his fall 1968 collection were the designer's good friends and clients Diana Vreeland, socialite and fashion icon C. Z. Guest, and the Duchess of Windsor (see fig. 62).[80]

For his 1969 resort collection, de la Renta looked back to his first contact with flamenco during his formative years in Spain, creating colorful dresses in polka-dot patterns and abstract prints saturated with color (fig. 21 and pls. 19–20). From short cocktail dresses to dramatic evening gowns with flamenco trains, the multitudes of ruffles gave a frenzied, joyous feel to the designs.

Austrian Symbolist painter Gustav Klimt was a muse of sorts for the fall 1969 collection (see fig. 22). De la Renta told *Women's Wear Daily*: "He [Klimt] has inspired many of my fall fabrics. What impresses me the most is how contemporary his color combinations are."[81] The collection was rooted in the turn of the twentieth century, with many of the silhouettes taking cues from Belle Époque fashion. It included high ruffled necklines for evening, the ruffles sometimes replaced by feathers for an extra flourish. Daytime looks were longer, often paired with capes instead of coats, but the effect was contemporary rather than historicizing. A double-breasted coat derived from menswear was given a youthful twist when paired with a short, matching jumpsuit.

De la Renta's innate talent, imagination, and the ability to push an idea in multiple directions allowed him to build on existing themes in his work to create collections that were constantly evolving. For fall 1970, Russia stimulated his imagination. The *New York Times* noted the audience's positive reaction after the fashion show, "What left everyone so limp was a parade of clothes that started with Penelope Tree modeling a prototype-peasant dress, complete with babushka [pl. 45] . . . and ended with beaded dresses inspired by Léon Bakst's costumes for the Diaghilev ballet."[82] *Women's Wear Daily* reported that de la Renta was inspired by the book *Journey into the Mind's Eye*, Lesley Blanch's autobiographical tale of her travels in search of a romanticized Russia.[83] The daywear received the most press. De la Renta used wool challis from Liberty of London that was printed with folkloric motifs in rich, dark colors. The

732

same patterns also could be found embroidered on a coordinating wool coat with fur collar. Of this grouping, de la Renta told *Women's Wear Daily*, which featured the coat ensemble on the front page, "they're on everybody's order."[84] Store buyers reported, "It was de la Renta's use of fabrics that told the most interesting and intriguing story of his fall offering."[85]

In a short documentary film from 1972, de la Renta explained his design process and the importance of textiles and color in conceiving his collections:

> Drawing is actually the way of starting a collection. I draw first and that is my way of creating. Once I start working on a collection, it takes me over three months of very intensive work. The beginning is always very difficult. Fabrics are very, very, very important for me, in fact, much more important than the drawings. Colors have a very, very special meaning and when I see a bolt of fabric, right away it is the color and the form and the design that says something to me. It is the color that helps me create and gives shape to things.[86]

He also spoke to the idea of being an American designer, but postulated that theoretically it is not where one is from or where one works, but the skill and vision each designer brings to the position—a fitting stance given his international background.

> I would say that in the world of design it is not a question of city or nationality, it is a question of personal talent. There are various designers working in Rome, Paris, London or New York and it is really the talent of the artist who gives luster to a city. . . . I consider myself an American designer because everything I have done and everything I have achieved, I have done and achieved in America.[87]

In 1973 de la Renta took part in a fashion show that pitted American designers against their French counterparts. The event, billed Le Grand Divertissement à Versailles (also known as the "Battle of Versailles"), was a fund-raiser for the Château de Versailles, where it took place (see fig. 23). It was the brainchild of fashion publicist Eleanor Lambert (of whom de la Renta was a client) and Gérald Van der Kemp, the chief curator at Versailles. Lambert wanted to promote American fashion in Paris, and Van der Kemp was desperately trying to raise money to restore the decaying palace.[88] As Lambert wrote to Marie-Hélène de Rothschild, a French socialite who would become a major organizer of the event, "If you have a charity, I have a crazy idea."[89]

The five designers chosen to represent France were Yves Saint Laurent, Hubert de Givenchy, Emanuel Ungaro, Pierre Cardin, and Marc Bohan for Christian Dior. The ready-to-wear designers Oscar de la Renta, Halston, Bill Blass, Anne Klein, and Stephen Burrows represented the Americans, and they were considered underdogs against France's greatest couturiers. The French went first, followed by the Americans, with each designer responsible for his or her own segment. Before the event de la Renta worried that Halston, who had a reputation for being difficult, would

25 Neal Barr. Dress of printed silk organza.
Originally published in *Harper's Bazaar*,
December 1970

demand to go last, and, in order to circumvent that inevitability, de la Renta rearranged the order of the lineup and claimed the final position for himself.[90]

With little time to prepare, de la Renta choreographed his own segment with models wearing pieces fresh off the runway from his spring 1974 collection (fig. 65).[91] The long, softly flowing chiffon and crepe de chine gowns were in a rainbow of pastel and sun-kissed colors and were notable for de la Renta's uncharacteristic lack of ornamentation. The ethnically diverse group of models walked to Barry White's "Love's Theme," with model Billie Blair acting as "fashion's mesmerizing magician," waving colored chiffon scarves—that she seemingly produced out of thin air—to cue models in the same hue to glide across the stage.[92] The *New York Times* wrote: "They [the models] have a cosmetic effect as they float around for evening in dresses that dip into handkerchief points, bare one shoulder or a lot of cleavage and look rather angelic."[93] The effect was subtle and ethereal, and de la Renta's finale elicited a standing ovation. He remembered, "No one had seen people move in that way. . . . There was some magic to it."[94]

In speaking about the 1970s, de la Renta stated, "I always say that I *survived* the seventies. What was really strong in fashion at that point, was not really what I did best."[95] But de la Renta did more than survive. He always designed for women's contemporary lifestyles and was committed to creating clothes that were adaptable to their ever-changing roles in society (see fig. 26). He was also an early advocate for the longer lengths that would dominate 1970s fashion (see fig. 25). By the end of the decade, his signature style of understated daywear and luxe evening dresses was back in vogue, as boldly proclaimed in a headline on the cover of *Women's Wear Daily* in 1978 that read, "High Chic-a-boom."[96] Below the headline was a photograph of four models wearing evening looks from Oscar de la Renta's resort collection (fig. 27). The image was used to illustrate the publication's pronouncement that "the return to extravagant entrance-making clothes leans heavily toward South American samba school chic."[97]

The following season de la Renta once again made the cover of the publication, with ten evening designs from his spring 1979 collection. He described the palette as "bold colors—black and white with ruby, sapphire or emerald."[98] One of the pieces was a playful update on a traditional black-and-white polka-dot flamenco dress for which he moved the flounce usually found at the bottom of the skirt to the neckline, where the white organza fell into soft folds that dipped dramatically in the back (pl. 25).

For his summer 1981 collection, de la Renta looked to the work of French artist Henri Matisse. De la Renta worked with textile designer Lisa Simmons to create colorful hand-painted silk caftans "in an odalisque mood inspired by Matisse's seminudes in an exotic Moroccan setting" (fig. 28). *Women's Wear Daily* aptly described the vibrant fabric, "the white silk crepe de chine fabric has gold, fuchsia, deep red and pink flat stylized flowers inside cobalt blue arabesque windows edged with a whimsical paisley border painted in marigold and cobalt blue on bright pink with an emerald outline."[99] The designs reflected de la Renta's expert eye for color and his ability to combine many vivid hues into an artistic expression that was uniquely his own.

26 Oscar de la Renta with models wearing looks from his fall 1972 collection on the sidewalk outside his home on East 62nd Street in New York

Colorful hand-painted floral caftans also appeared in his summer 1982 collection (see pl. 27). The large-scale prints featured Caribbean motifs such as tropical flowers, animals, and bold stripes in the bright sun-drenched colors of the islands. No added embellishment was necessary, as de la Renta let the prints be the focal point on these unstructured silhouettes.

Two months before his spring 1982 runway presentation, de la Renta told *Women's Wear Daily*, "I always design clothes in the romantic vein, of course, but I'd love to fabulously simplify what I do."[100] When speaking of that desired simplicity, he looked back on fashion history, invoking the names of designers Gabrielle "Coco" Chanel and Edward Molyneux.[101] He might have also added the name Elsa Schiaparelli in reference to the lavishly embellished evening dresses that acted as a striking counterpoint to much of the collection's pared-down aesthetic. The silk ball gowns were void of any decoration except for the bodices, which were each embroidered in the same brilliant golden sun motif, evoking the radiant sun embroidery of Schiaparelli's Cosmic collection of 1938–1939.[102] De la Renta, a great lover of history, was also referencing Louis XIV, the Sun King.

The eighteenth century of Marie-Antoinette was the starting point for a group of evening dresses for spring 1983. The dresses' silhouettes evoke the *chemise à la reine*, an informal type of dress made fashionable in the 1780s by the queen of France, who wore it in the gardens of the Petit Trianon at Versailles. The chemise dress was based on the undergarment of the same name, with a drawstring neckline that gathered into soft ruffles at the neck and a waist sash that provided definition to the otherwise unstructured gown. De la Renta's version was also a nod to eighteenth-century colors and motifs. In his hands the chemise dress was reconceived in silk organza printed in soft pastel floral patterns and trimmed with delicate lace (see pl. 56). The dresses called to mind a summer garden party, reminiscent of the setting where Marie-Antoinette would have worn the original.

In 1991 de la Renta made what was a bold move for an American designer: He decided to show his fall collection in Paris before it would be seen on the New York runway. In addition to the attendant publicity the fashion show would generate, there was also the prospect of significant financial gain, especially for his highly successful perfume, which was sold worldwide.[103] He explained his decision in an article published in *Mirabella*: "Today you want to have the world press and all the buyers in the world come and look at your collection. . . . You have to do it *there*."[104] By "there," of course, he meant Paris. The idea of becoming a global brand appealed to de la Renta's international sensibilities and business acumen. His plan included "new licensing arrangements; earlier shipments to the all-important markets in Japan and the United States; better manufacturing agreements abroad; and the launch of boutiques worldwide."[105] He went on to explain that one of the reasons he was pursuing an international business venture was that he recognized how "fashion is becoming a one-world market."[106] And he acknowledged its global reach, stating, "I'm an *international* designer. . . . Today, people—clothes—are international. Frontiers are non-existent."[107]

After the success of his first Paris fashion show, he returned the following season

to present his spring 1992 collection, an exuberant homage to his Dominican heritage (see figs. 29–30).[108] Caribbean themes permeated, from the tropical color palette to the crisp white linen daywear and the festive ruffled skirts and dresses in varying lengths and fabrications. Colorful head wraps completed the look. The dazzling collection was poignant in de la Renta's very direct references to some of his earliest memories. It was also a powerful statement that he, a Dominican-American designer, now had a foothold in the city where he had launched his career. As Bernadine Morris stated in her *New York Times* review, "No more gasps of amazement that an American dare show alongside the world fashion leaders. . . . In short de la Renta is accepted."[109]

The attention that his Paris showings attracted may have had an additional result: Just weeks before his spring 1993 collection debuted, *Women's Wear Daily* reported that de la Renta was "negotiating to become the couture designer for Pierre Balmain," which would be a prestigious and unprecedented appointment for an American ready-to-wear designer.[110] The paper reported that his collection "caused many to speculate that this was Oscar's public audition for the couture job" and that "the designer will spend the next few days in the French atelier, and if everything works out, he'll have a couture collection for Balmain in January."[111] By November it was official, and *Women's Wear Daily* announced de la Renta's new position with a photograph of him standing in front of the Arc de Triomphe in Paris. They called him "the Concorde Couturier," a direct reference to all the traveling he would be doing as a designer working in two countries.[112] During his tenure at Balmain, de la Renta continued to design his eponymous line, a groundbreaking move at the time, but not uncommon in today's global fashion industry.

Oscar de la Renta had a lot to offer Balmain, which, as he noted to Mower, "hadn't sold a single couture dress in two years."[113] He also brought with him a large following of loyal clients—an international list of the world's best-dressed women, many of whom were also couture devotees, such as Nan Kempner, Ann Getty, Mercedes Bass, Patricia Altschul, and Princess Marie-Chantal of Greece. In a CNN interview about his first Balmain collection, for spring/summer 1993, de la Renta neatly summed up how his own long-standing design philosophy meshed with that of the house's founder, Pierre Balmain:

> In designing this collection I spent a lot of time going through the archives and looking at every collection that Balmain designed . . . and what was extraordinary is that in trying to find out what the Balmain style was all about, I realized it had to do a lot with me, because Balmain didn't really mark a period of fashion in the same manner that perhaps some other designers did, but he certainly marked and created a sort of, very feminine clothes, elegant, for a true woman, you know, a *jolie madame*, and I thought perhaps this is what I have been doing all these years too, very feminine, very romantic clothes, so I thought there was a perfect marriage in the sense that my philosophy about designing clothes is not far from Balmain's own philosophy.[114]

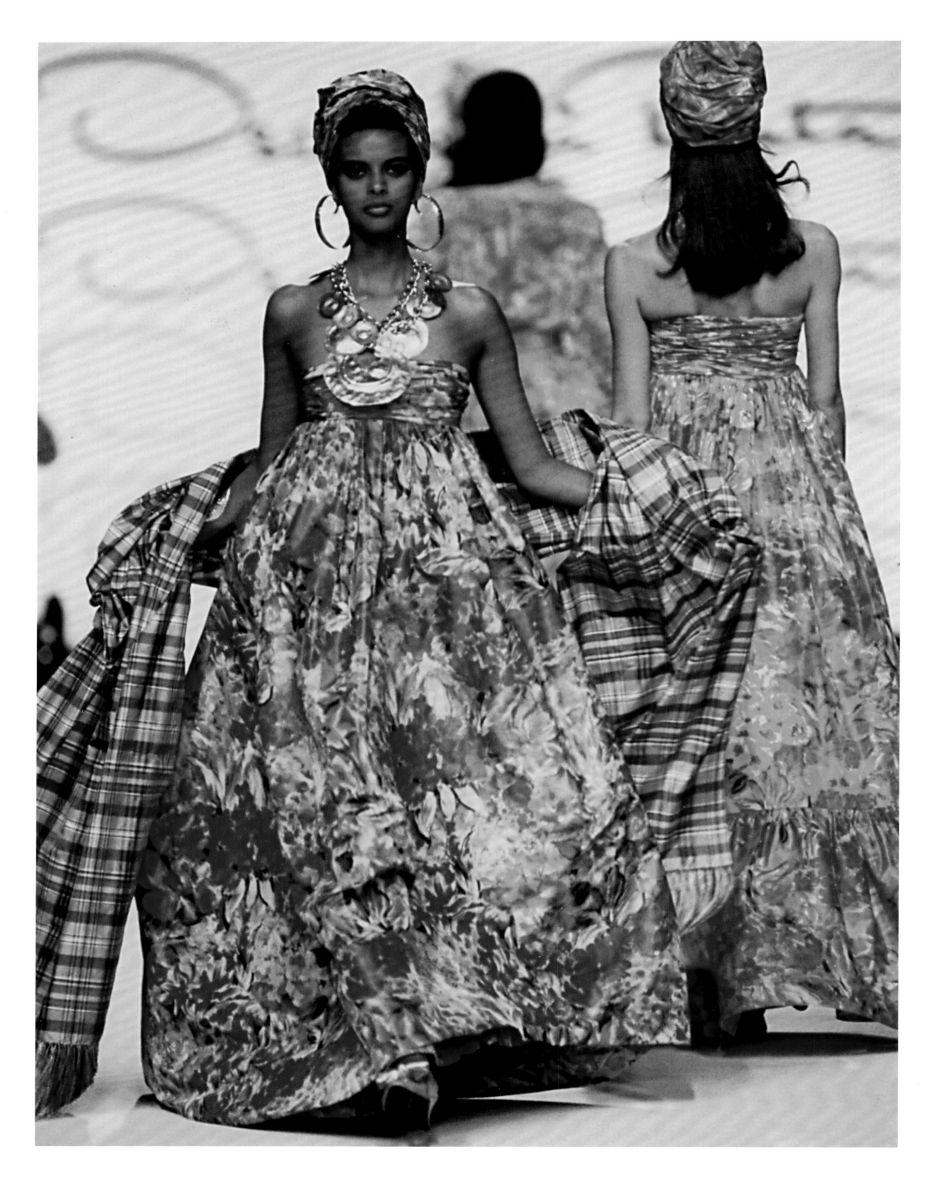

De la Renta came of age at a time when haute couture was less about fantasy and more about suitability to the occasion at which a garment would be worn, and was the only type of clothing women of certain means purchased. He maintained that philosophy during his tenure at Balmain, creating practical daywear of understated elegance and statement-making evening clothes that gave way to his most imaginative flights of fancy (see fig. 31) without ever reaching the extremes that would make them unwearable off the runway.

As a couturier working in Paris, de la Renta had access to the finest materials and craftsmanship to create clothing that was far superior in its construction and fit to anything available on the ready-to-wear market. For day he preferred skirts and pantsuits as well as coat-and-dress ensembles in double-faced cashmere or wool bouclé. For evening he embraced a heightened version of his historicizing and multicultural aesthetic. His beloved Spain could be found in Goyaesque black-lace cocktail dresses and evening pieces including a strapless jumpsuit and long coat that kept the wearer covered but left little to the imagination. References to flamenco could be found in a colorful floral-printed satin skirt with pleated ruffles (pl. 21), from autumn/ winter 2001–2001, and a white blouse paired with a black taffeta skirt that recalled the high-waisted, fitted trousers worn by male flamenco dancers. Even at his most minimal, de la Renta was capable of a subtle flourish, as with a slinky beige evening dress with a single decoration, a long fringe at the hem evoking the border of a Spanish shawl.

De la Renta revisited the eighteenth century for an evening ensemble of French blue–and–white striped taffeta in the style of a *robe à l'anglaise*, a dress with a fitted bodice and skirt that opened at the front to reveal the petticoat worn underneath (pl. 59, variant). In the version from his spring/summer 1998 collection, the petticoat was replaced by matching trousers, a modern update that gave the luxurious ensemble a more relaxed air and provided ease of movement for the wearer. The more formal *robe à la française*, characterized by a pleated panel that hangs from the back neckline to the hem and floats slightly away from the body, was the origin of two cocktail dresses from the same collection (pls. 61–62). The curved hiplines of the dresses also mimicked the silhouette created by the panniers worn under the *robe à la française*.

De la Renta was a master at creating subtly layered references. Looking to the East, he was inspired by Chinese dress, creating evening pajamas that followed a traditional silhouette. For autumn/winter 1999, one pair was trimmed in sable (pl. 38).

De la Renta's longtime love of textiles flourished at Balmain, where he had access to the highest quality fabrics, and embellishments such as embroidery. For spring/ summer 1997 he borrowed from the age-old ikat patterns of Uzbekistan and Turkistan, creating an evening ensemble consisting of a full-length coat and trousers (pl. 33). The shape of the coat followed a customary Uzbek design with full sleeves and skirt. Instead of using a conventionally produced ikat fabric, where the yarns are resist-dyed in a specific pattern before weaving, de la Renta mimicked the visual effect with luxurious silk embroidery, creating dimensional texture and an allover pattern that is virtually indistinguishable from conventional ikat unless one looks up close. The

visual splendor of the coat was enhanced by its colorful striped silk lining, a hidden detail only visible when the wearer moved.

Throughout his years at Balmain, de la Renta endlessly mined Russian culture, from humble folkloric embroideries to the opulence of imperial court dress and from religious iconography to literature. These potent influences were revealed in some of his most lavish eveningwear creations, including several from his autumn/winter 1997–1998 collection. De la Renta's romantic vision was revealed in a full-length fur-trimmed and stenciled silk velvet evening coat over striped taffeta trousers and a trio of floral satin ball gowns trimmed in sable (pls. 51–52).

The following year he zeroed in on Saint Petersburg, with the *New York Times*'s Amy Spindler calling his latest work "a gentle collection full of charm."[115] De la Renta's version of a Russian bride appeared in the finale of the couture runway show. Model Kylie Bax was dressed in a gold-embroidered silk taffeta evening gown that evoked both the ornately embellished and brocaded dresses of the imperial court as well as the motifs and coloration found on Russian religious icons.

De la Renta's tenure at Balmain ended with his autumn/winter 2002–2003 collection (see fig. 32). The day before the fashion show, his imminent departure was reported by *Women's Wear Daily*, which wrote that he was "eager to focus his energies on his fast-growing signature business in New York."[116] In her review of the show for the *New York Times*, Cathy Horyn wrote, "It was a wonderful show, not because the clothes represented such a departure but because they spoke so expertly to the knowing. And what a lineup: Deeda Blair; Cornelia Guest; two of the Miller sisters and their mother, Chantal; . . . Valentino."[117] Horyn continued, "Mr. de la Renta makes clothes to wear but they also give women confidence and stature."[118] The collection included strong Spanish and Russian themes as well as an evening ensemble consisting of a sleeveless blouse, the surface of which was completely covered in gilt cock feathers, and a skirt of pleated gold lamé (pls. 74–75). He considered this dress to be one of his finest creations, and "alluding to its divine qualities . . . named his creation after Minerva, the goddess of wisdom."[119] After loaning it to socialite Lee Radziwill, the younger sister of Jacqueline Kennedy Onassis, to wear to the Met Ball marking the opening of the exhibition *Goddess* at the Costume Institute at the Metropolitan Museum of Art, he donated it to the National Museum of American History at the Smithsonian.

After resigning from Pierre Balmain, de la Renta continued building his namesake brand and in 2004 opened his first store in the United States, a flagship on Madison Avenue in New York. And while he remained devoted to his longtime loyal clientele, he also developed a new following of young actresses, singers, and socialites, who embraced his day- and eveningwear designs for social and professional events including numerous walks down the red carpet. Actress Amy Adams wore Oscar de la Renta to the Academy Awards in 2013 (pl. 79). The following year singer Taylor Swift wore Oscar de la Renta to the Met Ball (pl. 81), and Rihanna performed onstage in an Oscar de la Renta evening dress in 2011.

For its December 2010 issue *Vogue* reimagined an iconic 1948 Cecil Beaton photograph of dresses designed by Charles James. In the new image by Steven Meisel, eight

models, all Asian, wear Oscar de la Renta ball gowns from the spring 2011 collection (pl. 58). The dresses include pastel taffetas, white lace, black ruffles, and floral embellishments—all de la Renta signatures. The picture illustrated a story about "a new crop of models from China, Japan and South Korea" that was "redefining traditional concepts of beauty."[120] Photographed in a drawing room that evoked a couture house setting, the image was about both the history and the future of fashion. De la Renta, who was inspired by the past but always looked forward, loved the photo.

Oscar de la Renta presented his last collection, for spring 2015, on September 9, 2014 (see fig. 12). In her review for the *New York Times*, Vanessa Friedman noted that "once upon a time, Mr. de la Renta was a couturier in Paris, and that experience in the atelier has never left him: he has respect for the classic forms (lunching suits, tea dresses, straight trousers—even full-blown ball gowns) that is almost palpable, not to mention an appreciation of the power of decoration and the allure it can bestow."[121] The fashion show was set against a backdrop of pink flowers that enhanced the garden-inspired collection of oversize ginghams, white lace, and delicate floral embroideries. Strapless evening dresses in de la Renta's favorite peacock silhouettes (short in front and long in the back) floated down the runway. For the past several years, he had returned to presenting his collection in his showroom, as he had in his earliest years on Seventh Avenue. In her review on Style.com, Nicole Phelps wrote, "The collection has hit all of Oscar's signature marks: feminine, unfailingly polished, lush with color. Less conventional perhaps was its youthful spirit."[122] De la Renta took his final bow flanked by models Daria Strokous and Karlie Kloss (p. 10 and fig. 68), who wrote on Instagram after the show, "There is no one on earth who makes a woman feel more beautiful than Oscar de la Renta."[123]

NOTES

(following spread)

34 Mert Alas and Marcus Piggott. Adele wearing an evening ensemble of marigold silk taffeta dress with a black floral-embroidered silk tulle overblouse. Originally published in *Vogue*, March 2012

1   Cathy Horyn and Enid Nemy, "Oscar de la Renta, Who Clothed Stars and Became One, Dies at 82," *New York Times*, October 20, 2014.

2   Fern Mallis, "Oscar de la Renta," in *Fashion Lives: Fashion Icons with Fern Mallis* (New York: Rizzoli, 2015), 247–248. This book contains Fern Mallis's full interview with de la Renta on June 6, 2013, part of her interview series at the 92nd Street Y in New York and the last in-depth interview with the designer before he died. Along with Sarah Mower's book (see note 3 below), it is the most thorough primary source material for biographical information about de la Renta.

3   Sarah Mower, *Oscar: The Style, Inspiration and Life of Oscar de la Renta* (New York: Assouline, 2002), 12, 15. Much of de la Renta's biographical information comes from Sarah Mower's excellent book about his life and career, which includes an extensive interview with the designer.

4   Mower, *Oscar*, 13.

5   Ibid., 16, 34; Mallis, "Oscar de la Renta," 248.

6   Mower, *Oscar*, 15–16.

7   Ibid., 16.

8   Ibid.

9   Ibid.

10 Mallis, "Oscar de la Renta," 253.

11 Oscar de la Renta, foreword to *Joaquín Sorolla and the Glory of Spanish Dress*, eds. Molly Sorkin and Jennifer Park (New York: Queen Sofía Spanish Institute, 2011), 13.

12 Mower, *Oscar*, 29.

13 De la Renta, foreword to *Joaquín Sorolla*, 13.

14 Mower, *Oscar*, 30.

15 Mower, *Oscar*, 21.

16 Ibid., 34.

17 Ibid.

18 See sketches by Ana de Pombo and Antonio del Castillo for Paquin in the collection of the Victoria and Albert Museum. Daniel Milford Cottam, "Paquin: Parisian Fashion Designs 1897–1954," *Victoria and Albert Museum* (blog), June 2, 2015, http://www.vam.ac.uk/blog/factory-presents/paquin-parisian-fashion-designs-1897-1954.

19 Mower, *Oscar*, 34, 39.

20 Ibid., 39.

21 Ibid.

22 Mallis, "Oscar de la Renta," 253.

23 Ibid.

24 *Life*, July 9, 1956.

25 Ibid., 117.

26 Mower, *Oscar*, 34.

27 Ibid.

28 Mower, *Oscar*, 40. Mower relates the story of de la Renta's job prospecting in Paris.

29 De la Renta, quoted in Mower, *Oscar*, 40.

30 Ibid.

31 Mower, *Oscar*, 44.

32 Ibid., 45.

33 Ibid.

34 *Women's Wear Daily*, February 21, 1962, 1.

35 "The Eye," *Women's Wear Daily*, November 21, 1962.

36 Ibid. De la Renta's name first appeared in *Women's Wear Daily* as Renta. He discussed his surname in Mallis, "Oscar de la Renta," 248.

37 Mallis, "Oscar de la Renta," 258.

38 Alfred Allan Lewis and Constance Woodworth, *Miss Elizabeth Arden: An Unretouched Portrait* (New York: Coward, McCann and Geoghegan, 1972), 302.

39 Ibid., 300. Since the departure of designer Count Ferdinando Sarmi, the Arden custom salons had offered interpretations of couture originals and used Carmel Snow, the former editor in chief of *Harper's Bazaar*, as their buyer. Snow purchased couture garments from well-respected French houses including Balenciaga and Lanvin-Castillo, and the Arden-produced interpretations were offered in both custom and ready-to-wear options. Gloria Emerson, "Feminine Enchantment Is Captured in Paris Adaptations," *New York Times*, March 8, 1960.

40 Lewis and Woodworth, *Miss Elizabeth Arden*, 302.

41 Mallis, "Oscar de la Renta," 257–258.

42 Ibid.

43 Ibid.

44 "The Eye," *Women's Wear Daily*, January 4, 1963, 8.

45 Mower, *Oscar*, 46.

46 Ibid.

47 "The Eye," *Women's Wear Daily*, January 9, 1963, 1.

48 "The Eye," *Women's Wear Daily*, January 10, 1963, 6.

49 *Women's Wear Daily*, January 11, 1963, 1.

50 "The Eye," *Women's Wear Daily*, January 10, 1963, 6.

51 "The Eye," *Women's Wear Daily*, January 11, 1963, 1.

52 Melissa Sones, "Oscar Goes Global," *Mirabella*, April 1991, 151.

53 "Two New Fashionables to New York," *Women's Wear Daily*, February 25, 1963, 5.

54 Ibid.

55 "Arden Shows Designs by de la Renta," *New York Times*, September 19, 1963.

56 Ibid.

57 Ibid.

58 *Women's Wear Daily*, October 2, 1963, 30.

59 Bernadine Morris, "Arden Styles Balance Austerity and Extravagance," *New York Times*, March 5, 1964.

60 Ibid.

61 Ibid.

62 Ibid.

63 "The Eye," *Women's Wear Daily*, April 13, 1964, 1.

64 Bernadine Morris, "Arden Fashions Are Sleek by Day, Lavish by Night," *New York Times*, February 18, 1965.

65 Mallis, "Oscar de la Renta," 259.

66 Ibid.

67 Ibid.

68 "Jane Derby Dead; Fashion Designer," *New York Times*, August 9, 1965.

69 "De la Renta's 7th Avenue Debut Is a Hit," *New York Times*, June 11, 1965.

70 Ibid.

71 Angela Taylor, "Coty's Winnie Given to Oscar," *New York Times*, June 30, 1967.

72 Foreword, Coty American Fashion Critics'
    Awards 1967, "Coty Awards 1967 Programs
    and Winners," Eleanor Lambert Records,
    Special Collections and College Archives,
    Gladys Marcus Library, Fashion Institute of
    Technology-SUNY.
73 Mower, *Oscar*, 64.
74 Script for the Coty American Fashion Critics'
    Awards 1967, "Coty Awards 1967 Programs
    and Winners," Eleanor Lambert Records,
    Special Collections and College Archives,
    Gladys Marcus Library, Fashion Institute of
    Technology-SUNY.
75 Eugenia Sheppard, "What's Ahead in Fall
    Fashion," *Des Moines* (IA) *Register*, June 13, 1967.
76 Ibid.
77 Marilyn Bender, "Coty Awards Are Voted to
    George Halley and Luba of Elite," *New York
    Times*, June 21, 1968.
78 Eugenia Sheppard, "Inside Fashion: Oscar's
    Arabian Nights," *Women's Wear Daily*, June 6,
    1968, 10.
79 "Master Designs for the Town and Country
    Woman," *Town and Country*, September 1968,
    122.
80 Eugenia Sheppard, "Inside Fashion: Oscar's
    Arabian Nights," *Women's Wear Daily*, June 6,
    1968, 10.
81 *Women's Wear Daily*, May 7, 1969, 1.
82 Bernadine Morris, "Fashions That Take the
    Focus Off the Hemline," *New York Times*, May 8,
    1970.
83 "Longuette for Fall: Oscar de la Renta," *Women's
    Wear Daily*, May 8, 1970, 5.
84 "De la Renta's Best Seller," *Women's Wear Daily*,
    May 14, 1970, 1.
85 "New Winner Chalked Up by de la Renta,"
    Women's Wear Daily, May 5, 1970, 37.
86 *Oscar*, 1972, Hearst Metrotone News, United
    States Information Agency.
87 Ibid.
88 Robin Givhan, *The Battle of Versailles* (New York:
    Flatiron Books, 2015), 82.
89 Eleanor Lambert, quoted in "Versailles,"
    Women's Wear Daily, October 16, 1973, 1.
90 Mallis, "Oscar de la Renta," 262.
91 Battle of Versailles, 192.
92 Ibid., 213.
93 Bernadine Morris, "The Idea Is Not To Be Kooky,
    and Not To Be Boring, Either," *New York Times*,
    October 31, 1973.
94 Givhan, *Battle of Versailles*, 213.
95 Sones, "Oscar Goes Global," 151.
96 "High Chic-a-boom," *Women's Wear Daily*,
    August 25, 1978.
97 Ibid.
98 "Renta's Night Flights," *Women's Wear Daily*,
    November 17, 1978, 1.
99 Margaret Mazzaraco, "Art by the Yard," *Women's
    Wear Daily*, February 18, 1981, 37.
100 Ben Brantley, "Slim and Simple, New York 1982,"
    Women's Wear Daily, September 30, 1981, 30.
101 Ibid.
102 For an image of the "Phoebus" cape from
    the Zodiac collection, see the Palais Galliera
    website: http://www.palaisgalliera.paris.fr/en/
    work/phoebus-cape-elsa-schiaparelli.
103 Sones, "Oscar Goes Global," 150.
104 Ibid.

105 Ibid.
106 Ibid.
107 Ibid., 149.
108 "Oscar's Boom-Boom Dress," *Women's Wear
    Daily*, October 22, 1991, 1.
109 Bernadine Morris, "Review/Fashion; Playing It
    Safe in Paris," *New York Times*, October 24, 1991.
110 Arthur Friedman, "Oscar, Balmain Talking about
    a Couture Line," *Women's Wear Daily*, October 6,
    1992, 1.
111 *Women's Wear Daily*, October 21, 1992, 8.
112 Kevin Doyle and Godfrey Deeny, "Oscar Sews
    Up Couture, RTW Deal at Balmain," *Women's
    Wear Daily*, November 17, 1992, 24. The Concorde
    was a supersonic jet in service from 1976 to
    2003 that flew transatlantic flights in less than
    half the time as regular airplanes.
113 Mower, *Oscar*, 184.
114 "Pierre Balmain Haute Couture Spring 1993"
    (includes an interview with Elsa Klensch
    for CNN Style), YouTube video, 2:25, posted
    February 7, 2015, https://www.youtube.com/
    watch?v=dt3FW5TaNlE.
115 Amy M. Spindler, "Fashion Review; Marking
    Time for the Millennium," *New York Times*, July
    28, 1998.
116 Miles Socha, "De la Renta to Exit Balmain,"
    Women's Wear Daily, July 8, 2002, 2.
117 Cathy Horyn, "Fashion Review; In Paris,
    Discipline, Decadence, and the Old Order
    Changes," *New York Times*, July 14, 2002.
118 Ibid.
119 "Treasures of American History: Creative
    Masterpieces, Minerva Dress by Oscar de la
    Renta," National Museum of American History,
    accessed August 6, 2015, http://american
    history.si.edu/treasures/creative-masterpieces.
120 Samantha V. Chang, "Asia Major," *Vogue*,
    December 2010, 299.
121 Vanessa Friedman, "As Old (and New) as Time:
    Michael Kors, Oscar de la Renta and More," *New
    York Times*, September 10, 2014.
122 Nicole Phelps, "Spring 2015 Ready-to-
    Wear, Oscar de la Renta," Style.com, posted
    September 9, 2014, accessed August 6, 2015,
    http://www.style.com/fashion-shows/
    spring-2015-ready-to-wear/oscar-de-la-renta.
123 Ibid.

JENNIFER PARK

Oscar de la Renta in *Vogue*

"American fashion has never been so sure of itself . . . the rhythm of perfection has taken over: here are the prettiest and most feminine clothes in the world— discretion by day, magic by night."[1]
—"*Vogue*'s Eye View: The New York Collections," a review including
   Oscar de la Renta for Jane Derby's first collection

ROMINENTLY DISPLAYED on the walls of Oscar de la Renta's office in New York were treasured prints of contemporary iconic images that featured the designer's work by some of the world's most renowned fashion photographers. Among them were Annie Leibovitz's photograph of Academy Award–winning actress Penélope Cruz in a crimson silk faille off-the-shoulder evening dress, commissioned for *Vogue*'s December 2007 cover (fig. 36); Mert Alas and Marcus Piggott's portrait of the critically acclaimed singer-songwriter Adele wearing a marigold silk taffeta gown with a black floral-embroidered silk tulle overblouse, shot for the March 2012 issue of *Vogue* (fig. 34); and Craig McDean's image of glamorous emerging models Cindy Bruna, Grace Mahary, and Imaan Hammam, each in a strapless multicolor jewel-tone silk taffeta dress, photographed for *Vogue*'s March 2014 edition (pl. 83). De la Renta celebrated the women he dressed by creating designs that reflected his romantic artistry, modern sensibility, and impeccable workmanship. Photography became an important vehicle through which his ideas on fashion were transmitted because it ultimately embodied the world of beauty that he hoped to create. Since its inception in 1892, *Vogue* has been a leading arbiter of style, chronicling fashion trends and reporting on significant developments within culture and society. For any creative working within the industry, a mention in the magazine has increasingly become a stamp of success. More than fifty years after Oscar de la Renta established his eponymous label, countless editorials and an impressive thirty covers of *Vogue* illustrate his lasting legacy in fashion.

From the very beginning of his career, Oscar de la Renta was recognized and championed by *Vogue* and its powerful editorial staff. Shortly after his arrival in New York from Paris, the designer made his notable first appearance in the magazine (figs. 37–38). *Vogue*'s issue of April 1, 1963, showed "The Clothes to Buy Right Now." Included among the looks were a white wool and cotton coat and a reversible cape of beige and white wool and camel's hair by Oscar de la Renta for Elizabeth Arden, both photographed by Louis Faurer. The caption heralded the "new talked-of young designer, a disciple of the great Castillo."[2] In referencing de la Renta's fashion heritage, the piece highlighted his training in the Parisian haute couture, which was evidenced in both garments in their thoughtful attention to fabric and construction. Oscar de la Renta's editorial prominence in *Vogue* spanned an unprecedented five decades and in many ways seemed preordained. In 1962 de la Renta came to New York with considerable letters of introduction: the astonishingly elegant Countess Jacqueline de Ribes (see fig. 23) recommended the budding designer to Diana Vreeland (see fig. 35), the mythical editor in chief of American *Vogue*, and French *Vogue*'s editor in chief Edmonde Charles-Roux presented him to Condé Nast's groundbreaking editorial director Alexander Liberman.

The year 1962 proved auspicious not only for Oscar de la Renta, but also for his two new acquaintances, who in time would become significant colleagues and devoted friends. While de la Renta made the radical decision to leave Paris in order to make his name in New York, Vreeland similarly contended with her own dramatic break: lured by Liberman, she made a sensational move to *Vogue* after twenty-five years as fashion editor of its chief rival, *Harper's Bazaar*. At *Harper's* Vreeland had made her legendary mark on fashion with her eccentric ideas on style and femininity. In her celebrated column "Why Don't You," she offered advice in the form of edicts on everything from what to wear to tips on interior design. Often abstract and beyond the realm of possibility for most of the magazine's readership, these concepts were meant above all to fuel the imagination.

A Russian émigré, Liberman was deeply influenced in his choice of careers by an event he attended in his youth, L'Exposition internationale des Arts décoratifs et industriels modernes, the World's Fair held in Paris in 1925,[3] where he was introduced to Constructivist examples of art, graphic design, and typography in the Russian Pavilion.[4] The Constructivist rejection of the autonomous work of art in favor of utilitarianism, and its relentless pursuit of experimentation were core principles that would ultimately inform Liberman's approach to art direction. He joined *Vogue*'s art department in 1941 and within two years was promoted to art director. He became editorial director of Condé Nast Publications in 1962, just before de la Renta arrived on the New York scene.[5] Liberman quickly put his imprint on *Vogue*, most prominently by shifting focus from fashion illustration to fashion photography. He recognized the medium's matchless ability to capture the imagination, stating, "The impetus to action through images is the power of the fashion photograph. The contemplation of a picture of a woman in a dress is an immediate invitation to a vicarious existence."[6]

It was Liberman's commitment to innovation against the backdrop of change looming at the start of the sixties that prompted his decision to court Vreeland. "From the moment she came to *Vogue*, she created a revolution," Liberman said. "Diana Vreeland shook up years of tradition that needed to be reexamined. She brought iconoclastic daring."[7] On the day of the announcement of her appointment as editor in chief, Vreeland spoke to *Women's Wear Daily* about the industry and fashion journalism's place in it:

(previous spread)

35 Oscar de la Renta with Diana Vreeland at his fashion show on March 3, 1976

(opposite)

36 Annie Leibovitz. Penélope Cruz wearing a custom red silk faille evening dress. Originally published on the cover of *Vogue*, December 2007

(following spread)

37–38 Louis Faurer. Coat of white wool and cotton, and hat of brown balibuntal straw (left), and reversible cape of white wool and beige camel hair, and hat of beige leather (right), Elizabeth Arden by Oscar de la Renta. Originally published in *Vogue*, April 1, 1963

39 Helmut Newton. Evening dress of sky-blue silk faille with crystal-bead embroidery, Elizabeth Arden by Oscar de la Renta. Originally published in *Vogue*, October 1, 1964

40 Helmut Newton. Evening dress of grass-green silk and metallic brocade, Elizabeth Arden by Oscar de la Renta. Originally published in *Vogue*, October 1, 1964

(*this spread*)

42 Henry Clarke. Evening dress of ivory silk crepe, Oscar de la Renta for Jane Derby. Originally published in *Vogue*, December 1, 1965

(*following spread*)

43 Henry Clarke. Day dress of printed jersey. Originally published in *Vogue*, June 1, 1967

44 Henry Clarke. Day ensemble of tunic and shorts of white linen. Originally published in *Vogue*, June 1, 1967

of the most unforgettable images in the history of fashion photography. From the beginning, Penn's photographs were marked by a severe formalism that reflected his unrivaled skill at still-life photography. By meticulously orchestrating composition and lighting, he captured frozen moments in time that placed a primacy on the clothing—the model was merely a symbol. As Penn stated, "I don't think the girl's personality should ever intrude."[11] With astute precision, he highlighted the unique aspects of each ensemble, which proved essential when it came to showcasing the lavish details of de la Renta's work. In a 1966 photograph of an Oscar de la Renta for Jane Derby brown double-faced wool coat, for example, the model Wilhelmina poses with her left hand on her hip and her right knee slightly raised (pl. 11).[12] The coat falls back on itself on one side, and on the other the pushed-up sleeve reveals the interior facing—both intentional gestures that serve to emphasize the reverse fabric in ivory wool that otherwise would not have been seen. In the issue of September 1, 1967, a vibrantly colored printed caftan by Oscar de la Renta is photographed on a model in repose. Her hand placement accentuates the garment's main attraction, the stone-embellished cuffs and pockets. The designer's first appearance on *Vogue*'s cover, in January 1967—a graphic purple jersey dress with white stripes for Jane Derby—was shot by Penn. Several years later on the cover from November 1, 1971, Karen Graham wears a signature dramatic flamenco-inspired de la Renta black silk taffeta halter dress. A single pop of color, a crimson rose fastened at the base of the model's neck, is the focal point of Penn's photograph (pl. 18).

Whereas Irving Penn preferred the sanctity of the studio, where he could control each variable, Diana Vreeland encouraged photographers to shoot on location in order to explore the world around them and share that view with *Vogue*'s readers. She shrewdly realized that the fantasy of the fashion editorial provided an escape for those who could not afford the glamorous trips to far-flung places promised by the golden age of travel. As Nancy Hall-Duncan explained in her early history of fashion photography:

> A fashion photograph does not depend on realism, yet one of the most convincing reasons that it is a potent selling device—more so than a drawing or a sketch—is our willingness to believe it. No matter how artificial the setting and despite our awareness that every fashion shot—even a realistic one—is posed and orchestrated, a photograph persuades us that if we wear these clothes, use this product or accessorize in such a way, the reality of the photograph will be ours.[13]

When asked about the state of fashion photography in 1962, Vreeland proclaimed, "You have to keep on moving."[14] She sent her photographers to North Africa, the Middle East, India, South America, and even in pursuit of gypsies in Spain. As Liberman's biographers Dodie Kazanjian and Calvin Tomkins recount:

> Vreeland once told Irving Penn to go to Spain and photograph a gypsy queen who "bathed in milk and had the most wonderful skin in the world." As Penn

45 Henry Clarke. Dresses of printed silk organza. Originally published in *Vogue*, June 1, 1969

told the story later, he "chased gypsies all over Spain," and "not only was there no queen, but they rarely bathed, let alone in milk." I came back and told Mrs. Vreeland that I hadn't been able to find the gypsy queen, and she looked at me and said, "What gypsy queen?"[15]

Beyond the literal, what Vreeland sought was something intangible. She imparted conceptual dictums and left their interpretation to the artist. More often than not, the search to find a solution became the relevant journey.

As a young man Oscar de la Renta made his own trek across southern Spain. He was swept up in a gypsy caravan on his way to join the Romería de El Rocío, a renowned pilgrimage in homage to the patron saint of the Andalusian village of Almonte. He later explained, "The sights, sounds, and drama of Spanish culture . . . were burned forever in my imagination, defining my own aesthetic."[16] The epiphany helped create de la Renta's distinct fashion signature, which reflected his multiculturalism and joie de vivre. Flamenco ruffles, matador embellishments, vibrant colors, luxurious textiles, religious iconography, and fine art were constant sources of inspiration in his collections. Though born in the Caribbean, de la Renta completed his formal training in Europe, where his sensibility was informed by centuries of European history and luxury. The fashion press took note and christened him with such epithets as the "Couture Conquistador" and the "Sultan of Suave."[17]

These honorifics were given life in some of *Vogue*'s most arresting fashion stories that were dreamt up by Vreeland and shot by Henry Clarke. For the June 1969 issue, Vreeland dispatched Clarke to Spain and invited readers to experience "clothes with a twinkle in their eye, bursting with energy, fizzing with fantasy . . . thrashes of color and gleam that lighten the mood, turn up the glow."[18] Exuding "the gypsy spirit," two Oscar de la Renta printed silk organza dresses were worn by models on "a two-seater donkey for a clop through Seville" (fig. 45).[19]

De la Renta also was linked to the exoticism of the East, once being hailed as the "Guru of Glamour."[20] "Match Me Such Marvel! A Rhapsody on Middle Eastern Themes," a stunning twenty-two-page editorial in the December 1965 issue, included "fashions on the sun and shimmer theme."[21] The majestic opening spread—photographed by Clarke on location against the ancient ruins of Palmyra in Syria—featured a vision of a goddess in an ivory silk crepe halter dress by Oscar de la Renta for Jane Derby (fig. 42). Two years later Vreeland sent Clarke and "the *Vogue* caravan" to Udaipur, India, "to this city of dreams . . . bearing fashion for the whole world's summer."[22] Rajput murals and stone monuments of spirited animals provided the backdrop for a story that highlighted three designs by Oscar de la Renta: a white linen tunic worn to accentuate "sandaled legs, long and burnished"; a "sun-orange" flocked cotton and rayon paneled dirndl dress; and a jersey dress printed with a "sun mosaic of blue, yellow, and pink swirled arabesques"[23] (figs. 43–44).

Susan Train, then the Paris editor of American *Vogue*, said of Henry Clarke, "One of his greatest gifts was doing his homework. He knew all about the places we were going, and he was able to tell the official guides assigned to us, 'No I want this

46 Richard Avedon. Penelope Tree with Briolette of India diamond, New York, July 8, 1967

and this,' and we would race around the country with two models, a hairdresser and a fleet of cars."[24] Clarke began in the prop department of Condé Nast studios in the late 1940s. He eventually earned a scholarship to the New School for Social Research, where the visionary Alexey Brodovitch taught his seminal course, Design Laboratory.[25] Brodovitch was the longtime art director of *Harper's Bazaar*, and his pioneering work set the visual standard for fashion magazines in the first half of the twentieth century. In Design Laboratory, students were taught to consider the dialectic between image and text in the "graphic approach to the printed page."[26] The class became a launching pad for influential photographers such as Lillian Bassman, Hiro, Diane Arbus, Garry Winogrand, and Art Kane, to name a few. Illustrious alumni also included Irving Penn and Richard Avedon—arguably the two most important fashion photographers of the twentieth century.

In 1966 Richard Avedon followed Diana Vreeland from *Harper's Bazaar* to *Vogue*, and together they developed "an image of a new kind of woman," a fresh-faced alternative to the prim and manicured ideal of the fifties, represented by the likes of Twiggy, Penelope Tree, and Jean Shrimpton.[27] At *Harper's*, Vreeland and Avedon had already collaborated on archetypal fashion photographs that would come to define the golden age of couture. When he began at *Vogue*, Avedon created images located "firmly in the 1960s," by revisiting one of his early obsessions, the investigation of movement, an apt theme for the swinging sixties.[28]

The year before Avedon's arrival at *Vogue*—and the same year that de la Renta began at Jane Derby—Vreeland had announced the arrival of a new cultural movement, the Youthquake: "More dreamers. More doers. Here. Now. Youthquake 1965."[29] Hastened by a new wave of British music, the Youthquake recognized the young as an independent style force. It channeled their energy and spirit, and, most importantly, their desire not to dress like their parents. For American audiences, Vreeland's interpretations tastefully introduced the Youthquake to *Vogue*'s more conservative readership. "That was something," said Vreeland, "a top, a bare midriff, and a belly button showing. The letters came in. 'This is a house where magazines are put on the coffee table, and now we find it impossible to put *Vogue* there.'"[30] It was the perfect moment for Oscar de la Renta, who excelled at translating the youth vibe for the ladies who lunched. De la Renta's designs embodied his notion of the modern woman. He explained, "It is understanding their lifestyle, understanding their aspirations, and understanding their dreams, and making them dream—that's what it takes to make clothes."[31] And it is the job of fashion photographs then to translate this sentiment. As legendary stylist Polly Mellen elaborated, "They convey the flavor of the moment; and these flavored moments together constitute the taste of their age."[32]

The model Penelope Tree was introduced in a 1967 editorial, envisaged by Polly Mellen (then Devlin) and photographed by Richard Avedon. The title of the story, "The Penelope Tree," posited her as the new "It Girl." As Mellen explained, "She projects the spirit of the hour, a walking fantasy, an elongated exaggeratedly-huge-eyed beautiful doodle drawn by a wistful couturier searching for the ideal girl."[33] Tree was the personification of an alternative beauty that fascinated Avedon (see fig. 46).

Liberman observed, "He likes women with character and women with allure, and he's interested in discovering fresh visions of beauty."[34] The essay included an Oscar de la Renta ensemble consisting of a tunic and shorts in black silk crepe and turtleneck jewels, with matching jeweled boots. That same year, when de la Renta won his first Coty American Fashion Critics' Award—the industry's top prize at the time—he said that had been inspired by "the flower children, hippies, Afghan coats, Thea Porter, who did beautiful caftans, and all those designers in London."[35] Several years later the designer featured Penelope Tree on the runway in a peasant-inspired look that was part of his best-selling fall 1970 collection (pl. 45). In a memo from 1970, Vreeland remarked of de la Renta's clothes, "Each and every costume has such beautiful balance. He has, like Dior, Givenchy and Saint Laurent, a total head-to-toe look and this is so vitally important."[36]

By the mid-sixties, a distinctly American youth subcultural movement had grown from the seeds of Youthquake. The summer of 1967 was the Summer of Love. Tens of thousands of flower children or "hippies," as they became known, attended the Monterey International Pop Festival, which included such headliners as The Jimi Hendrix Experience, The Who, Janis Joplin, and Ravi Shankar. In his exposé of San Francisco's Haight-Ashbury neighborhood, the hippie capital, for the *New York Times,* writer Hunter S. Thompson defined a hippie as "someone who 'knows' what's really happening, and who adjusts or grooves with it. Hippies despise phoniness; they want to be open, honest, loving and free. They reject the plastic pretense of the 20th-century America, preferring to go back to the 'natural life,' like Adam and Eve."[37] Thompson further noted, however, that just as quickly as the group appeared, their look was co-opted, repackaged, and then sold to the thousands of tourists flocking to the "Hashbury," as he dubbed it.[38] *Vogue*'s idealized version of "hippiedom" appeared in the issue of April 15, 1968, with "Heroine's All—A Romantic Charade Starring Jean Shrimpton."[39] Shot by Avedon, the editorial showed Shrimpton in a diaphanous Oscar de la Renta silk chiffon evening dress wreathed in roses (fig. 47). Also in 1968, de la Renta was honored with his second Coty Award, completing an extraordinary back-to-back achievement. Resonating with the late-sixties hippie aesthetic, the designer increasingly became known for his floral prints and dazzling smashes of color, exemplified by his spring 1969 "giant-flowered print" jumpsuit, photographed by Raymundo de Larrain with a psychedelic kaleidoscope effect (fig. 48).

Flower power began to fade with the arrival of the seventies. By 1971 events such as the Charles Manson murders and the release of the Pentagon Papers, which sparked large-scale, angry protests against the Vietnam War, set a troubling tone for the decade. A more ominous mood inescapably infiltrated fashion, which was reflected in editorial. Richard Avedon, in his eternal quest for alternative beauty, turned his lens on a new muse: "Anjelica Huston. Dark and mysterious as a raven, remote and graceful as a medieval heroine—a beauty . . . is passionate about long Isadora scarfs, and walks under every ladder she sees."[40] Her haunting look was embodied in an Avedon image from 1970: Huston, in cornrows and exaggerated eye makeup, is a "little white lamb," wearing a one-sleeved, fringed shawl of Swakara by Oscar de la Renta Furs (fig. 49).[41]

The Story of

THE BARENESS
THE FRAGRANCE

everyone gets the message

No question. The look of the moment is the look of skin—bare summer skin, tinted lightly by sun, showing silkily through cutaway backs and fronts and sides and middles. And smelling delicious . . . a hint of jasmine rising from the plunge of a neckline . . . clean, tingly traces of citrus lingering coolly in the curve of an arm . . . clouds of mimosa spinning in the air when a woman turns her back on a dance floor. Evocative, provocative, fragrance is the touch that rounds out the fashion, makes it personal . . . and sweet to all the senses. . . . On these pages, the whole day-and-night gamut of summer bareness: the clothes, the fragrances . . . the possible consequences.

Bare arms, bare neckline, *left*— Oscar de la Renta's cinnamon halter-smock for day. To wear with six smooth wooden bangles . . . and ardent splashes of eau-u-u. (Clearly, one person here hasn't got the message yet; never mind, on the next page, the spectator catches up with the sport.) . . . Dress, of polyester and cotton, about $90. Lord & Taylor; Nan Duskin; Martha, Palm Beach, Bal Harbour; Godchaux's; Balliet's; I. Magnin. His watch, Cartier. Everything here, and on the following 12 pages, photographed at St. Tropez, in and around La Paziella, the house built for Elsa Martinelli and her husband Willy Rizzo by Roger Herrera. The mood throughout heightened by the hair-and-make-up wizardry of Rick Gillette.

For more stores carrying Fragrances with a Fashion Message, see page 178.

Ohhh....

HELMUT NEWTON

(Continued) thing to do there is buy it. Failing that, one could always sell oneself. All the intervening actions seem superfluous, there is only buying and selling. Those who understood and acted upon the first urge were Sir Basil Zaharoff, the armaments baron, and Aristotle Onassis. Both sought and acquired controlling shares in the S.B.M., the Société des Bains de Mer, which controls the casinos and the hotels. Both lost their control and retreated. Those who understood the latter urge were Cleo de Mérode, La Belle Otéro, and Liane de Pougy, those Belle Époque actresses who were known as *"Les Grandes Horizontales."* It was Otéro who said, "No man with an account at Cartier can be called really ugly," and her pragmatic spirit survives there to this day.

Although there are now a hundred reasons besides gambling to go to Monte Carlo—such as the Grand Prix, the Bal de la Croix Rouge, endless young Greeks bearing gifts, a glimpse of the beautiful Princess Caroline, the circus competition—the most satisfying act one can commit there is the spending of money. This is easy in the hotels, easy in the   *(Continued)*

TO CATCH
A DIAMOND...

MONTE CARLO: DINNER. THE HÔTEL DE PARIS. LA BELLE ÉPOQUE. VOLUPTUOUS NYMPHS. CARYATIDS. A STRANGER WATCHES . . . THE DIAMONDS

FAR LEFT

<u>The diamonds:</u> *From Harry Winston, a necklace of 76 oval-shaped stones totaling 62.94 carats; perfectly matched heart-shaped earrings totaling 16.5 carats*

<u>The model:</u> *Rosemary McGrotha*

<u>The fashion:</u> *Oscar de la Renta*

NEAR LEFT

<u>The diamonds:</u> *Harry Winston's chandelier earrings—35.93 carats of pear-shaped stones; a flawless 30.99 carat emerald-cut ring, slightly pink in color; 26-carat bracelet of square stones*

<u>The model:</u> *Eva Wallen*

<u>The fashion:</u> *Ungaro couture*

Details, next to last pages

Helmut Newton

267

A new sense
of color....At
Oscar de la Renta,
the enchantment of
fantasy color...
brilliant prints...
ruffled harlequins
...dazzling gold...
dreams within
dreams in
a glorious
spectacle of color

opulent clothes, which were my thing."[61] The success of Turbeville's depictions of de la Renta's designs are rooted in their conflicted juxtapositions: the beautiful women wearing extravagantly fashionable clothing are completely isolated and disconnected from the world around them (see fig. 54). This paradox defined the decade of excess. Extreme wealth as portrayed in Oliver Stone's *Wall Street* (1987) potently illustrated the rise of multinational corporations in the 1980s. The technology sector boomed, and against that backdrop in popular culture, a revolution in music called MTV came about. The disparity of global economic distribution, however, fueled the political unrest that shaped much of the Cold War era. World-shattering events such as the Tiananmen Square protests and the fall of the Berlin Wall, both in 1989, rounded out the decade.

If Deborah Turbeville offered a world of mystery and turmoil, Arthur Elgort was just the opposite. He stated, "What's important in this business is giving the public a dream they can relate to."[62] Elgort's first photographs were of ballet dancers, both on and off the stage. The more candid shots of girls before and after the spotlight— what he called the "snapshot kind of thing"—would become his trademark in fashion photography.[63] Alexander Liberman declared, "With Arthur Elgort a new era opened up of marvelous American young women caught in action, going about their lives. This is what fashion magazines are all about today—the sense of purpose in a modern woman's life."[64]

Working in plein air, Elgort took models outside the studio and embraced spontaneity. For example, "Born in the U.S.A." a February 1992 editorial that followed supermodels Christy Turlington and Naomi Campbell around New Orleans as it explored the country's influence on fashion that season, included a spread featuring Oscar de la Renta's designs, which coincidentally celebrated the designer's love of music (fig. 55). His two ensembles—a cap-sleeved dress and double-breasted suit—were fittingly shot in a jazz café as legendary musician Ellis Marsalis (father of Wynton and Branford) played piano to Campbell's upright bass. Elgort's frequent collaborator, the lauded creative director Grace Coddington, described one of his most extraordinary moments for *Vogue*: "We took Linda Evangelista to Scotland where, despite the inclement weather, Arthur's humor never waned. Running outside between rain showers he was able to capture instances that only the speediest of lensmen could achieve—Linda, dressed in immaculate Oscar de la Renta, tossing a caber or kicking a bagpiper" (fig. 56).[65]

Bookending the famous Elgort editorial were two milestones in de la Renta's career: in 1990, the year prior to the publication of the image, he was awarded the Council of Fashion Designers of America's (CFDA) Lifetime Achievement Award, and in 1992 he began work on his first haute couture collection for the house of Pierre Balmain, becoming the first American to design for a French couture house. *Vogue* praised de la Renta's successful tenure at Balmain in its coverage of the couture collections. For instance, "Ravishing Couture," shot by Elgort, included an enchanting photograph of Audrey Marnay as the "Belle de Jour," wearing a voluminous pink silk taffeta skirt and a crisp linen blouse from the haute couture spring/summer 1999 collection (pl. 54). The contrasting fabrics demonstrated de la Renta's genius at "merging old-world grandeur with all-American ease."[66] The designer acknowledged the new, modern couture client and astutely recognized fundamental changes occurring within the industry. De la Renta observed, "It is a very different scene in the nineties than it was in the sixties. Balmain once employed eight hundred people, and now there are a maximum of forty-five working on the couture. So there had to be a new relevance, something a woman with a certain lifestyle could relate to."[67]

Visually inventing a fashionable way of life has been a hallmark of the work of Patrick Demarchelier. Current editor in chief of *Vogue* Anna Wintour noted that "Patrick was one of the very first photographers to make the connection between fashion and lifestyle; his pictures convey how a woman interacts with style and the stylish world around her."[68] In editorials such as "Venetian Holiday," Demarchelier created a world in which "*Roman Holiday* meets the Venice Film Festival," where supermodel Christy Turlington—styled in multiple Oscar de la Renta daywear looks by the irreverent fashion editor Carlyne Cerf de Dudzeele—is "the starlet who just wants to see the sights" (fig. 57).[69] Like his contemporary Elgort, Demarchelier mastered shooting outdoors and on location. The rise of supermodels in the 1990s was charted by their appearance in ubiquitous, now iconic fashion photographs that were often the work of Demarchelier.

For *Vogue*, the nineties marked the ascent of Wintour, who would continue to revolutionize the magazine into the twenty-first century. At the time of her appointment in 1988, S.I. Newhouse Jr., the head of Condé Nast Publications, revealed his desire to revamp *Vogue* for the upcoming decade, stating, "The change in the 1990s, when we look back, will be as decisive as the shift from the 60s to the 70s."[70] The rise of the World Wide Web transformed media and communications during the nineties. The trials and tribulations of Generation X, also called the "MTV Generation," played out on screen in films such as Richard Linklater's *Slacker* (1991) and Ben Stiller's *Reality Bites* (1994). Grunge and hip-hop dominated youth culture.

Wintour's prescient turn toward popular culture ushered in an increasingly diverse audience for *Vogue*. During her reign, the roster of global leaders, Hollywood stars, and influential socialites that Oscar de la Renta dressed only grew. It was a list that included bold-faced names such as former first lady Laura Bush (see pl. 82), Queen Rania of Jordan, Nancy Kissinger, Jayne Wrightsman, Barbara Walters, Nicole Kidman, Renée Zellweger, Gwyneth Paltrow, Carey Mulligan, Nicki Minaj, Rihanna, and many more. Most appeared in the magazine wearing de la Renta's designs and photographed by the likes of Steven Klein, Nick Knight, Peter Lindbergh, Steven Meisel, David Sims, Mario Testino, and Bruce Weber.

In the increasingly celebrity-driven world of fashion, Testino has emerged as one of the most sought-after portraitists. Anna Wintour declared, "He adores women, adores celebrity—and they adore him right back."[71] Sarah Jessica Parker, longtime muse to de la Renta, was photographed by Testino for *Vogue* on several occasions. In the August 2011 issue, she appeared not only on the cover of the magazine shot by Testino, but in an extended story that featured a photograph of the actress in a sequin embroidered white silk faille evening dress by de la Renta (pl. 26). Testino's multicultural roots—Peruvian born, London based—have become relevant in a highly

(following spreads)

55 Arthur Elgort. Christy Turlington wearing a dress of white wool and Naomi Campbell wearing a suit of white wool. Originally published in *Vogue,* February 1992

56 Arthur Elgort. Linda Evangelista wearing a coat of plaid wool. Originally published in *Vogue,* September 1991

globalized world. In his glamorous editorials, where he hopes to make women "look their best," he explores not only idealized beauty, but the exotic locales that these beauties find themselves in.[72] For *Vogue*'s September 2012 issue, Testino returned to his native Peru to shoot model Stella Tennant, as styled by Camilla Nickerson, in a "richly embellished wardrobe as luxe as the fabled treasures of the Incan empire."[73] The editorial included a photograph of Tennant, wearing an Oscar de la Renta ensemble of silk tulle with sequin and paillette embroidery, strolling Lima's Calle de Pescadería with two llamas (fig. 58).

For women, the nineties marked a third wave in feminism. While the Spice Girls were espousing "girl power" on stage through song, significant advancements simultaneously were being made in politics. In 1991 the US Department of Labor established the Glass Ceiling Commission to eliminate barriers for qualified women in the workplace. In 1992, a year heralded as the "Year of the Woman," the US Senate welcomed four female senators to its ranks. During the nineties the country saw the first woman US attorney general, Janet Reno, and the first woman US secretary of state, Madeleine Albright. Hillary Rodham Clinton became the first former first lady to be elected to the US Senate, in 2002. All three pioneering figures were featured in *Vogue*. Clinton appeared on the December 1998 cover wearing a burgundy velvet evening dress by Oscar de la Renta and photographed by Annie Leibovitz. A crowning achievement for de la Renta, it was the first time in the magazine's history that a first lady appeared on the cover.

Years later, in 2013, the Clinton Presidential Center commissioned an exhibition of the designer's work to celebrate his fifty years in fashion. On the occasion of the show, Anna Wintour commented on the secret of de la Renta's success: "Any great designer will have a point of view and a look and a very strong signature . . . and that's what Oscar has. . . . I think most of all you look at the girl and then you say, 'Oh she's very Oscar.'"[74] From the very beginning of his career as represented on the pages of *Vogue*, Oscar de la Renta's evolution was consistently rooted in his strong sense of self and in the identity of the women he was designing for. He stated, "I have observed how women in the last forty to fifty years have crossed barriers that were unthinkable. I am lucky that I am a part of that movement to understand the power of a woman."[75] De la Renta was always looking forward and forever in fashion—a legacy immortalized in the unforgettable images that have featured his work in *Vogue*. Alexander Liberman asserted, "Whatever their pictorial or creative value, *Vogue*'s photographs retain a vital historical importance. This documentary value is one of the unique contributions of fashion photography to the memory of civilization."[76] These photographs attest to Oscar de la Renta's gift for making designs that are at once timeless and reflective of the changing image of women over the past five decades. They irrefutably establish him as a creative giant that stood a world apart from his peers.

NOTES

1 "*Vogue*'s Eye View: The New York Collections," *Vogue*, September 1, 1965, 193.
2 *Vogue*, April 1, 1963, 136.
3 Francine du Plessix Gray, *Them: A Memoir of Parents* (New York: Penguin, 2005), 118.
4 Robert W. Rydell, *World of Fairs: The Century-of-Progress Expositions* (Chicago: University of Chicago Press, 1993), 67.
5 Dodie Kazanjian and Calvin Tomkins, *Alex: The Life of Alexander Liberman* (New York: Alfred A. Knopf, 1993), 135–136.
6 Polly Devlin, *Vogue Book of Fashion Photography, 1919–1979* (New York: Simon and Schuster, 1979), 7.
7 Quoted in Amanda Mackenzie Stuart, *Empress of Fashion: A Life of Diana Vreeland* (New York: HarperCollins, 2012), 190.
8 "The Fashion Chief," *Women's Wear Daily*, November 30, 1962, 4.
9 Sarah Mower, *Oscar: The Style, Inspiration and Life of Oscar de la Renta* (New York: Assouline, 2002), 79. For more on de la Renta's career at Elizabeth Arden, see Sorkin essay in this volume.
10 *Vogue*, November 15, 1963, 92.
11 Quoted in Martin Harrison, *Appearances: Fashion Photography Since 1945* (New York: Rizzoli, 1991), 56.
12 De la Renta left Elizabeth Arden in 1965 to pursue his dream of a ready-to-wear collection. The new venture, Oscar de la Renta for Jane Derby, became simply Oscar de la Renta two years later, upon Derby's death.
13 Nancy Hall-Duncan, *The History of Fashion Photography* (New York: Alpine, 1979), 10.
14 "The Fashion Chief," 4.
15 Kazanjian and Tomkins, *Alex*, 236.
16 Molly Sorkin and Jennifer Park, eds., *Joaquín Sorolla and the Glory of Spanish Dress* (New York: Queen Sofía Spanish Institute, 2011), 13–16. For more on de la Renta's years in Spain, see Sorkin essay in this volume.
17 Fern Mallis, *Fashion Lives: Fashion Icons with Fern Mallis* (New York: Rizzoli, 2015), 247.
18 *Vogue*, June 1, 1969, 82.
19 Ibid., 84–85.
20 Mallis, *Fashion Lives*, 247.
21 *Vogue*, December 1, 1965, 180.
22 *Vogue*, June 1, 1967, 83.
23 Ibid., 97–99.
24 Quoted in Enid Nemy, "Henry Clarke, 77, Photographer of High Fashion for Magazines," *New York Times*, May 5, 1996.
25 Hall-Duncan, *History*, 225.
26 Kerry William Purcell, *Alexey Brodovitch* (New York: Phaidon, 2002), 75.
27 Harrison, *Appearances*, 138.
28 Ibid.
29 *Vogue*, January 1, 1965, 112.
30 Mackenzie Stuart, *Empress of Fashion*, 200.
31 "Oscar de la Renta Spring 2009" (includes an interview with Linda Fargo), YouTube video, 4:04, posted by Bergdorf Goodman, January 9, 2009, https://www.youtube.com/watch?v=IQG07ShFpg0.
32 Devlin, *Vogue Book*, 113.
33 Polly Devlin, "The Penelope Tree," *Vogue*, October 1, 1967, 163.
34 Kazanjian and Tomkins, *Alex*, 244.

35 Mower, *Oscar*, 89.
36 Ibid., 92.
37 Hunter S. Thompson, "The 'Hashbury' Is the Capital of the Hippies," *New York Times*, May 14, 1967.
38 Ibid.
39 *Vogue*, April 15, 1968, 56–57.
40 *Vogue*, September 15, 1969, 123.
41 *Vogue*, November 1, 1970, 143.
42 Michael Gross, "War of the Poses: *Bazaar*'s New Liz Takes on *Vogue*'s Anna," *New York Magazine*, April 27, 1992, 29.
43 Ibid., 30.
44 Grace Lichtenstein, "Feminists Demand 'Liberation' In *Ladies' Home Journal* Sit-In," *New York Times*, March 19, 1970.
45 Ibid.
46 *Vogue*, February 1, 1971, cover.
47 *Vogue*, June 1978, 145.
48 *Vogue*, July 1, 1971.
49 Helmut Newton, "The Eyes of Helmut Newton," *New York Magazine*, December 4, 1978, 12.
50 Jesse McKinley, "Helmut Newton Is Dead at 83," *New York Times*, January 25, 2004.
51 *Vogue*, May 1975, 102.
52 *Vogue*, December 1979, 264.
53 *Vogue*, February 1975, 117.
54 Jessica Iredale, "Fashion Photographer Deborah Turbeville," *Women's Wear Daily*, October 28, 2013, 7.
55 Angela Taylor, "The Deborah Turbeville Look: Altering the Focus on Fashion," *New York Times*, January 24, 1977.
56 Hall-Duncan, *History*, 231.
57 Harrison, *Appearances*, 250.
58 Taylor, "Deborah Turbeville Look," 27.
59 *Vogue*, February 1980, 227.
60 Ibid., 230–231.
61 Mower, *Oscar*, 97–98.
62 Margo Jefferson, "The Art and Business of Courting the Camera: *Arthur Elgort's Models Manual*," *New York Times*, July 6, 1994.
63 Harrison, *Appearances*, 262.
64 Ibid., 260.
65 Arthur Elgort, *Arthur Elgort's Models Manual* (Göttingen, Germany: Steidl, 2014), n.p.
66 *Vogue*, March 1999, 382–383.
67 Mower, *Oscar*, 184.
68 Patrick Demarchelier, *Patrick Demarchelier* (Göttingen, Germany: steidlDangin, 2008), n. p.
69 *Vogue*, December 1990, 248–263.
70 Woody Hochswender, "Changes at *Vogue*: A Complex Tale of Rumors and Facts," *New York Times*, July 25, 1988.
71 Suzy Menkes, "Mario Testino at 30 Years," New York Times, October 2, 2011, http://www.nytimes.com/2011/10/03/fashion/03iht-rma-ri003.html?_r=0.
72 Ibid.
73 *Vogue*, September 2012, 764.
74 Anna Wintour, interview in Richard Kaufman, *Oscar de la Renta: American Icon*, documentary film produced for the William J. Clinton Presidential Center, Little Rock, Akansas, 2013.
75 Oscar de la Renta, interview in Kaufman, *Oscar de la Renta*.
76 Devlin, *Vogue Book*, 23.

(opposite)

58 Mario Testino. Stella Tennant wearing an ensemble of embroidered silk tulle. Originally published in *Vogue*, September 2012

(followng spread)

Patrick Demarchelier. Oscar de la Renta with Jacquetta Wheeler wearing a cocktail dress of sequin-embroidered champagne silk tulle and silk satin. Originally published in German *Vogue*, June 2005

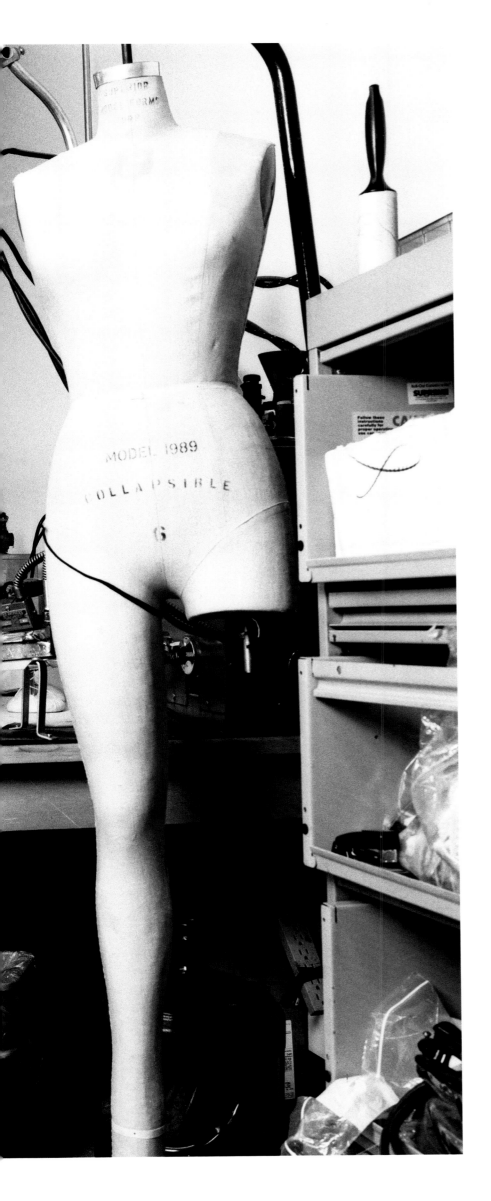

PLATES

BEGINNINGS

"I believe that my sole purpose as a designer is to create something that I think a woman would want to wear."

—Oscar de la Renta (*Oscar*, 1972)

FROM THE VERY BEGINNING of his illustrious career, Oscar de la Renta's focus was on designing beautiful clothes for every occasion of a woman's life. After training and working in Europe for more than ten years, de la Renta moved to New York in 1963 to become the designer for Elizabeth Arden's line of made-to-order clothing. His success was immediate, and in 1965 a *New York Times* headline lauded him for designs that were "sleek by day, lavish at night" (Morris, 1965), an apt description that would characterize his work for the next fifty years. New York's rapidly growing ready-to-wear industry initially drew de la Renta, and he transitioned to it in 1965 when he began working for Jane Derby, an established firm that would soon become his eponymous line. His earliest work included jaunty yet sophisticated daywear and evening clothes that ranged from the understated elegance of an asymmetrical column dress and a softly flowing bias-cut gown to evening pajamas in lively floral patterns and lavishly embellished cocktail and evening gowns, often in sumptuous brocades—all hinting at what would become his signature style. During a time when women's roles in society were rapidly evolving, de la Renta's designs were worn and promoted by society's most influential and discerning arbiters of style including Diana Vreeland, *Vogue*'s editor in chief and one of his initial champions.—MS

(previous spread)

1 Irving Penn. Cocktail dress of black silk crepe and white satin with galloon edging and bead embellishment, fall 1968. Originally published in *Vogue*, September 1, 1968

2 House sketch of evening dress of printed silk cloqué and Lurex, with rhinestone appliqué, fall 1967

3 House sketch of jumpsuit with flounced overskirt of printed silk organza, fall 1969

4 Evening dress of azure-blue silk, spring 1974

#5-40

(this spread)
5 House sketch of dress of yellow cotton and synthetic *matelassé* with metallic ribbon and bead appliqué, summer 1967
6 House sketch of evening dress of crepe, fall 1967

723

(following spread)
7 House photograph of dress of black double-faced satin, Elizabeth Arden by Oscar de la Renta, autumn/winter 1963
8 House photograph of day ensemble of a wool jacket and skirt, Elizabeth Arden by Oscar de la Renta, autumn/winter 1963

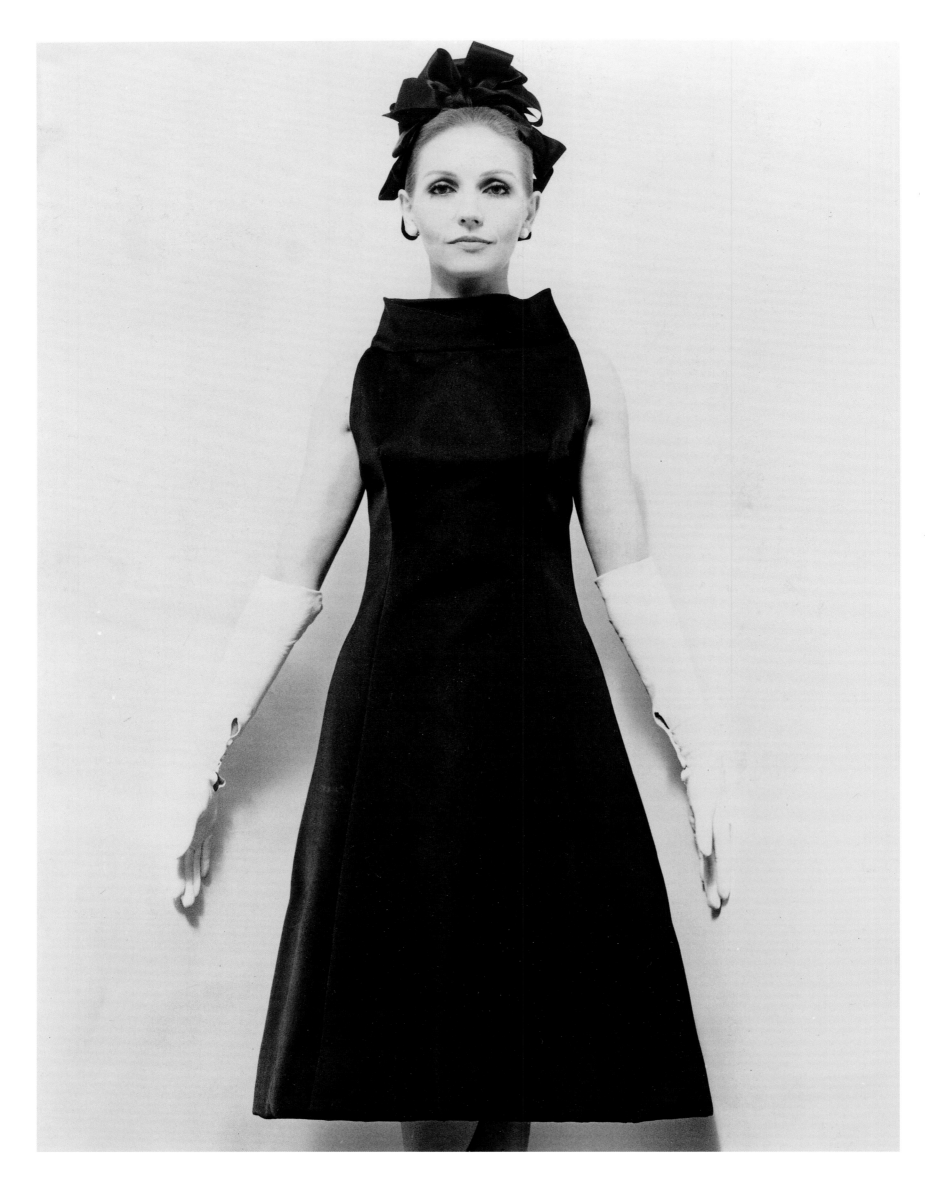

134—

yellow +
wht.

9 House sketch of day ensemble of dress and jacket of yellow and white wool,
Oscar de la Renta for Jane Derby, fall 1966

207 —

10 House sketch of day ensemble of dress and jacket of yellow and green plaid synthetic fabric,
Oscar de la Renta for Jane Derby, fall 1966

11 Irving Penn. Wilhelmina wearing an ensemble of coat of brown double-faced wool and a dress of ivory wool,
Oscar de la Renta for Jane Derby, spring 1966. Originally published in *Vogue*, March 15, 1966

132

SPAIN

"What I saw in Spain colored the way I have looked at clothes ever since."

—Oscar de la Renta (Mower 2002, 30)

OSCAR DE LA RENTA WAS DEEPLY INSPIRED by the people, customs, and history of Spain. He began his career in fashion at the couture house of Cristóbal Balenciaga in Madrid, where he was hired to sketch existing designs for prospective clients. Like Balenciaga, de la Renta would come to draw on the spectacle and pageantry of Spanish culture, and references to its fine art, flamenco, bullfighting, and festive celebrations recur in his collections. The designer marveled at the country that produced one of the most important golden ages of art. From the jewel tones of the sacred paintings of El Greco and Francisco de Zurbarán to the extraordinary depictions of court costumes and royal armor in the portraits of Diego Velázquez, allusions to Spanish art consistently appeared in the silhouettes and ornamentation of his designs. An early encounter with the celebrated flamenco dancer Pilar López also left an indelible mark on de la Renta's oeuvre, in the form of lively patterns and cascading ruffles. In the 1960s de la Renta traversed Andalusia to see all of the matches of one of Spain's greatest bullfighters, Antonio Ordóñez, the matador chronicled in Ernest Hemingway's *The Dangerous Summer*. The elaborate tassels and embroideries of bullfighting attire often materialized in de la Renta's creations, as did the colors of the matador's cape, fuchsia on one side and saffron yellow on the other, two of the most enduring hues that appeared season after season. Likewise, the brilliant costumes created from luxurious fabrics he saw at traditional festivities such as the *ferias* of Seville were imprinted permanently on his aesthetic.—JP

(previous spread)

12 Mario Testino. Dress of embroidered white silk organza and organza appliqué, fall 2000. Originally published in *Vogue*, December 2000

13 Cape of saffron-yellow and fuchsia silk satin, Oscar de la Renta for
Pierre Balmain, autumn/winter 1993–1994

16 Evening coat of red double-faced cashmere and wool, silk faille, and jet embroidery,
Oscar de la Renta for Pierre Balmain, autumn/winter 1999–2000
17 Dress of white silk tulle and silk taffeta, spring 2005

18 Irving Penn. Evening dress of black silk taffeta, fall 1971. Originally published in *Vogue*, November 1, 1971

731

22 Evening dress of sequin and bead embroidered black silk crepe, fall 1996

23 Evening dress of black silk velvet and rhinestones, Oscar de la Renta for
Pierre Balmain, autumn/winter 2000–2001

24 Sheila Metzner. Cocktail dress of printed silk taffeta, fall 1986. Originally published in *Vogue*, November 1986
25 Dress of black-and-white polka-dot silk chiffon with flounce of white silk gazar, spring 1979

26 Mario Testino. Sarah Jessica Parker wearing a dress of silk faille with sequin embroidery, resort 2012.
Originally published in *Vogue*, August 2011

ASIA

"I have always been attracted to the exotic, no question about it . . . I would always look at folklore and how people were dressed in different cultures . . . that's what fascinates me."

—Oscar de la Renta (Mower 2002, 89)

THROUGHOUT HIS CAREER Oscar de la Renta looked to cultures from around the world for inspiration for his couture and ready-to-wear pieces. The rich and complex history of the geographical region spanning the Middle East to the Far East, and including North Africa and Turkey, emerged as a starting point in the conceptualization of many of de la Renta's most romantic collections. He was one of a long line of couturiers who injected exoticism into Western fashion. In the early twentieth century, Paul Poiret frequently evoked the Ottoman Empire, where every element of sultanate dress revealed rank and position within society. Later, Cristóbal Balenciaga created sculptural day suits and evening dresses that referenced the simple lines and sumptuous fabrics of East Asian traditional dress. De la Renta succeeded this legacy with his own signature versions inspired by harem pants, caftans, cheongsams (or *qipaos*), and kimonos. Further, the lavish embroideries found in Chinese textiles, the colorful woven ikat patterns of India and Uzbekistan, vibrant Japanese prints, and lush Persian paisleys have been particularly fertile sources for his textile surface designs.—JP

(previous spread)
27 Caftan of hand-painted silk crepe de chine, summer 1982
(opposite)
28 Coat of printed silk velvet with fox trim, fall 2013

158

Oscar de la Renta
Oscar de la Renta
Oscar de la Renta
Oscar de la Renta
Oscar de la Renta
Oscar de la Renta
Oscar de la Renta
Renta
Renta
Renta
Renta
Renta
Renta
Renta

29 Evening ensembles of jackets of silk velvet and bead embroidery, and pants of silk, fall 1988

30 Evening ensembles of tunics and pants of printed silk, metallic lace, and cording, fall 1982

31 Steven Meisel. Coat of silk warp-resist dyeing (ikat), spring 2005.
Originally published in *Vogue*, April 2005

32 Caftan of polychrome silk blend, Oscar de la Renta for Pierre Balmain, spring/summer 1997

33 Evening ensemble of coat of polychrome silk embroidery and silk taffeta, and pants of turquoise silk shantung, Oscar de la Renta for Pierre Balmain, spring/summer 2000

34 Irving Penn. Evening ensemble of tunic and pants of jade green wool, silk, and Lurex with galloon banding, fall 1968.
Originally published in *Vogue*, September 1, 1968

35–36 Evening dress of embroidered silk and cornflower-blue silk taffeta,
Oscar de la Renta for Pierre Balmain, autumn/winter 2002–2003

37 Evening ensemble of tunic and pants of sapphire-blue silk velvet and silk chiffon
hand-painted in metallic gold and green, fall 1997

38 Evening ensemble of tunic of embroidered red silk crepe de chine and pants of black silk velvet and sable tails,
Oscar de la Renta for Pierre Balmain, autumn/winter 1999–2000

39 Irving Penn. Dress of printed brocade, Oscar de la Renta for Jane Derby, resort 1967.
Originally published in *Vogue*, January 1, 1967

172

40 Evening ensemble of tunic of black silk velvet with gold silk appliqué and pants of black silk velvet,
Oscar de la Renta for Pierre Balmain, autumn/winter 1999–2000

41 Evening ensemble of top and skirt of metallic brocaded silk, Oscar de la Renta for
Pierre Balmain, autumn/winter 1999–2000

RUSSIA

"Magical stories about Russia . . . fed my imagination and made me dream."

—Oscar de la Renta (Mower 2002, 13)

THE *NEW YORK TIMES* STYLE SECTION announced "The Return of the Babushka" in 1995, which also marked the thirtieth anniversary of the film version of the epic melodrama *Doctor Zhivago*, starring Omar Sharif and Julie Christie. By the mid-nineties, Oscar de la Renta had already been at the helm of Pierre Balmain for several seasons, designing lauded haute couture collections that were often inspired by a romanticized Russia. Luxurious furs, ornate textiles, jeweled appliqué, embroidered trims, and even such accessories as Cossack hats were odes to the opulent aesthetic of Saint Petersburg. De la Renta's earliest industry recognition—the Coty Award in 1967—was won for a collection that included such Russian motifs as exquisite brocaded gowns trimmed in fur, recalling the court of Catherine the Great, and printed tunics with a folkloric twist. For his hugely successful fall 1970 collection, the designer sent Penelope Tree down the runway in a babushka and a peasant-inspired dress. That same season, de la Renta dreamt up shimmering beaded evening dresses that recalled Léon Bakst's costumes for Diaghilev's Ballets Russes. From the tumultuous history of the Russian empire to its crowning artistic and literary achievements, de la Renta continually mined references from the country's vast cultural heritage.—JP

(previous spread)

42 Evening ensemble of dress of black silk velvet with over-bodice of gold lace and rhinestone embroidery, fall 1984

43 Oscar de la Renta fitting an evening ensemble of a jacket and skirt of printed silk
and bead and sequin embroidery, fall 1989

44 Ensemble of jacket of burgundy silk moiré faille with gold and bead appliqué and gold lace trim, top of burgundy
and gold lace, and skirt of burgundy plaid silk taffeta (right), fall 1981

45 Penelope Tree on the runway in a coat of black wool with paisley and fox-fur trim, fall 1970

(opposite)

(following spread)

(opposite)
46 Ensemble of blouse of orange and metallic striped silk chiffon, and skirt of raspberry silk gauze, spring 1982

(following spread)
47 Oscar de la Renta with models wearing evening looks during the finale of his spring 1982 fashion show

558

Sable Trim

48 Evening dress of polychrome lamé, sable, and metallic braid, fall 1968
49 House sketch of evening dress of polychrome lamé, sable, and metallic braid, fall 1968

50 Evening coat of metallic stenciled olive-green silk velvet and sable, Oscar de la Renta for
Pierre Balmain, autumn/winter 1997–1998

51 Evening ensemble of coat of metallic stenciled silk velvet and sable, and pants of brown striped silk taffeta,
Oscar de la Renta for Pierre Balmain, autumn/winter 1997–1998

GARDEN

"A garden is the most spiritual and pure of joys. . . . It's a communion with nature and beauty in the most simple and fundamental form."

—Oscar de la Renta (Mower 2002, 163)

OSCAR DE LA RENTA was a lifelong gardener whose passion for all things horticultural began at a young age, when he was given a small area to plant and tend at his childhood home in the Dominican Republic. Growing up he was surrounded by the vibrant colors and sweet fragrances of hibiscus, tuberose, and ylang-ylang (Mower 2002, 13) that flourished in the bright sunlight of his tropical surroundings. Much later he was renowned for the gardens he created at his homes in the Dominican Republic and Connecticut, the latter where he created a more formal landscape in perfect harmony with natural vistas. "Gardeners and couturiers possess many of the same talents," his friend Rosemary Verey wrote with de la Renta in mind, "imagination, knowledge, and industry. Both know which colors shock or coordinate, which textures rasp or soothe, and both see fashions change—but they never forget that the concept of beauty is timeless" (Bowles 2008, 318). Botanical themes abounded in de la Renta's work, from floral-printed silk taffetas to delicately appliquéd flowers and soft ruffles that evoked petals in full bloom. He also looked to the eighteenth century of Marie-Antoinette for silhouette, pattern, and color; one can easily imagine many of these dresses in the gardens of the Petit Trianon at Versailles. Great gardeners, like great designers, layer colors and textures to create worlds of unimaginable beauty, as reflected in de la Renta's creative output in both realms.—MS

(previous spread)

54 Arthur Elgort. Evening ensemble of blouse of pink linen and skirt of pink silk taffeta, Oscar de la Renta for Pierre Balmain, spring/summer 1999. Originally published in *Vogue*, March 1999

196

55 Evening ensemble of overdress of sky-blue and white-striped silk taffeta,
and pants of gold silk taffeta, spring/summer, 1999

56 Ensembles of blouses and skirts of printed silk organza and belts of silk satin ribbon, spring 1983
57 Evening ensemble of blouse and shawl of white silk organza, and skirt of white silk organza with polychrome silk embroidery,
Oscar de la Renta for Pierre Balmain, spring/summer 2000

(previous spread)

58 Steven Meisel. *Asia Major* with Liu Wen, So Young Kang, Du Juan, Lily Zhi, Bonnie Chen,
Hyun Lee/SILENT models NY, Tao Okamoto, Hyoni Kang/FORD Model. Evening dress of chartreuse silk faille;
evening dress of black silk taffeta and *point d'esprit* lace; evening dress of ivory silk faille, silk tulle,
and silk satin ribbon; evening dress of pink silk organza, eggshell cord embroidery, and pink silk faille; evening
dress of salmon-pink silk faille; evening dress of gray silk taffeta and black silk tulle; evening dress of
pale-pink and gold silk organza and gold lamé; and evening dress of green silk faille and pink and green silk
embroidery and appliqué, all spring 2011. Originally published in *Vogue*, December 2010

(opposite)

59 Evening ensemble of overdress and pants of sky-blue and white-striped chiné silk taffeta,
Oscar de la Renta for Pierre Balmain, spring/summer 1998

(following spread)

60 Annie Leibovitz. Kirsten Dunst wearing a custom evening dress of blue-and-white chiné silk taffeta, 2006.
Originally published in *Vogue*, September 2006

61 Cocktail dress of floral-printed silk taffeta, Oscar de la Renta for
Pierre Balmain, spring/summer 1998

62 Cocktail dress of floral-printed silk taffeta, Oscar de la Renta for
Pierre Balmain, spring/summer 1998

63 Patricia Canino. Evening dress of green-and-white striped silk taffeta, Oscar de la Renta for Pierre Balmain, spring/summer 1994
64 Evening dress of green-and-white striped silk taffeta, Oscar de la Renta for Pierre Balmain, spring/summer 1994

65 Evening dress of embroidered jade-green silk with sable trim, Oscar de la Renta for
Pierre Balmain, autumn/winter 2000–2001

66 Evening dress of pale-pink silk tulle, Oscar de la Renta for
Pierre Balmain, spring/summer 1997

BALLROOM

"What I try to do in my design is to make a woman dream."

—Oscar de la Renta (Fargo 2009)

OSCAR DE LA RENTA'S SOARING VISION for eveningwear exudes luxurious romance, and his designs are the ultimate expression of femininity and elegance. His technical mastery of dressmaking is on full display in both his ready-to-wear and couture creations—from a ball gown seemingly conjured from clouds of tulle to a molded bodice delicately constructed out of gilt cock feathers to a dress of pleated shimmering lamé that recalls ancient Greece. Velvet is molded into a figure-hugging column, and a ball gown is inspired by a nineteenth-century silhouette. The fantasy imbued in de la Renta's work is embraced by the world's most recognizable women, from first ladies to actresses to pop stars, who dominate the red carpet in his evening dresses. Devoted clients Hillary Rodham Clinton and Laura Bush both wore his designs to their husbands' second inaugurations as well as to state dinners they hosted at the White House. In 2011 singer-songwriters Rihanna and Nicki Minaj accepted music awards wearing de la Renta dresses fresh off the runway. Amy Adams reigned on the red carpet at the 2013 Academy Awards wearing a gown of tulle ruffles with a regal train, while Taylor Swift dazzled at the 2014 Met Ball in an embroidered petal-pink silk organza dress. Sarah Jessica Parker, who wore de la Renta to the same event, has said admiringly of the designer, "He makes you think you are his only customer" (Reed 2004).—MS

(previous spread)
67 Craig McDean. Evening dresses of silk tulle, fall 2012

68 Penélope Cruz wore an evening dress of black silk and silk tulle from the fall 2012 collection to the *Alexander McQueen: Savage Beauty*
Costume Institute Gala at the Metropolitan Museum of Art in New York on May 2, 2011

69 Gladys Perint Palmer. Fashion illustration of an evening dress of black silk velvet with white silk embroidery and appliqué,
Oscar de la Renta for Pierre Balmain, autumn/winter 1999–2000

70 Evening dress of black silk velvet with white silk embroidery and appliqué, Oscar de la Renta for
Pierre Balmain, autumn/winter 1999–2000

(this spread)

71 Peter Lindbergh. Evening dress of violet silk faille and metallic embroidery, fall 2013

72 Evening dress of violet silk faille and metallic embroidery (left) and evening dress of fuchsia silk faille and metallic embroidery (right), fall 2013

(following spread)

73 First Lady Hillary Rodham Clinton wore a custom evening ensemble of a dress and wrap of printed chiné silk taffeta from 2000 on September 17, 2000, for the India State Dinner Honoring Prime Minister Atal Bihari Vajpayee

219

74–75 Evening dress of silk, gold lamé, and gilt cock feathers, Oscar de la Renta for Pierre Balmain, autumn/winter 2002–2003.
Originally published in *Vogue*, December 2002

(opposite)

76 Patrick Demarchelier. Evening dress of burgundy silk velvet and silk satin, fall 2006.

Originally published in *Vogue*, August 2006

(following spread)

77 Annie Leibovitz. Evening dress of pleated silver lamé, pre-fall 2012.

Originally published in *Vogue*, June 2012

224

78 Jessica Chastain wore an evening dress of pleated silver lamé from the pre-fall 2012 collection to the British Academy Film Awards at the Royal Opera House in London on February 12, 2012

79   Amy Adams wore a custom evening dress of pale-blue silk tulle from 2013 to the 85th Academy Awards
at the Dolby Theatre in Hollywood on February 24, 2013

80 Sarah Jessica Parker wore a custom evening dress of white duchesse satin and silk velvet from 2014 to the *Charles James: Beyond Fashion*
Costume Institute Gala at the Metropolitan Museum of Art in New York on May 5, 2014
(following spreads)
81 Taylor Swift wore a custom evening dress of pink silk organza with silk and bead embroidery from 2014 to the *Charles James: Beyond Fashion*
Costume Institute Gala at the Metropolitan Museum of Art in New York on May 5, 2014
82 First Lady Laura Bush wore an evening ensemble of silk tulle and bead and sequin embroidery from the spring 2002 collection
for the Poland State Dinner honoring President Aleksander Kwaśniewski on July 16, 2002

86 Jonathan Becker. Brooke de Ocampo wearing an evening dress of red silk taffeta, fall 2005. Originally published in *Vogue*, September 2005

87 Evening dress of emerald-green silk taffeta and black Battenberg lace, spring 2012

88 Evening dress of white silk faille with red and green silk embroidery and appliqué, resort 2012

89 Diane B. Wilsey wearing an evening dress of green silk tulle, black lace, and silk satin, resort 2006

(following spread)

90 Annie Leibovitz. Kate Moss wearing an evening gown of champagne silk tulle and ribbon and sequin embroidery, fall 2009.
Originally published in *Vogue*, May 2009

2000   Wins the CFDA Womenswear Designer of the Year Award.

Marches as the grand marshal in New York's Hispanic Day Parade.

Receives the Gold Medal for Merit in Fine Arts from the king of Spain.

2001   Introduces accessories collection, which includes handbags, belts, shoes, and jewelry.

2002   Launches home collection.

2004   Launches retail division with the opening of a flagship store on Madison Avenue in New York.

Launches eyewear collection.

Appointed chairman of Queen Sofía Spanish Institute, New York.

2005   First Lady Laura Bush wears Oscar de la Renta designs for the second inauguration of President George W. Bush.

2006   Launches bridal collection.

Receives the Lifetime Achievement Award at Parsons School of Design's 58th Annual Benefit and Fashion Show.

2007   Is corecipient of the CFDA Womenswear Designer of the Year Award.

2008   The company opens its first international retail stores in Madrid and Athens, Greece.

2010   Conceives and leads the *Balenciaga: Spanish Master* exhibition at Queen Sofía Spanish Institute, New York.

2011   Conceives and leads the *Joaquín Sorolla and the Glory of Spanish Dress* exhibition at Queen Sofía Spanish Institute, New York.

2012   Introduces childrenswear line.

        Conceives and leads the *Fortuny y Madrazo: An Artistic Legacy* exhibition at Queen Sofía Spanish Institute, New York.

2013   Receives the CFDA Founders Award, given in honor of Eleanor Lambert.

        Oscar de la Renta: American Icon opens at the William J. Clinton Presidential Center, Little Rock, Arkansas.

2014   Receives the Medal of Excellence from Carnegie Hall in New York City.

        Cochairs the Met Ball at the Metropolitan Museum of Art's Costume Institute in New York City.

        On October 20, dies at home in Connecticut surrounded by family, friends, and his dogs.

Checklist of the Exhibition

All works are by Oscar de la Renta under his own label, unless otherwise noted.

All Oscar de la Renta works for Pierre Balmain are haute couture.

This list is arranged chronologically under each thematic section and reflects the most complete information available at the time of publication.

All photographs featured in this section are by Robert Fairer.

BEGINNINGS

Elizabeth Arden by Oscar de la Renta

Evening ensemble; dress and jacket, autumn/winter 1963–1964

Fuchsia peau de soie, sable trim

Chicago History Museum, 1967.9ab

Elizabeth Arden by Oscar de la Renta

Evening coat, ca. 1964

Peach silk satin

Museum at the Fashion Institute of Technology, 79.147.2

Worn by Diana Vreeland

Oscar de la Renta for Jane Derby

Coat, resort 1966

Rhinestone-studded Comark vinyl

Phoenix Art Museum, 1975.C.226

Oscar de la Renta for Jane Derby

Dress, resort 1966

White synthetic net, foil and plastic embroidery, silver metallic trim

Rhode Island School of Design Museum, 1987.075.3

Oscar de la Renta for Jane Derby

Day ensemble; dress and jacket (pl. 9), fall 1966

Yellow and white wool

Kent State University Museum, Gift of Oscar de la Renta, 1986.33.32 a–c

Oscar de la Renta for Jane Derby

Day ensemble; dress and jacket (pl. 10), fall 1966

Yellow and green plaid synthetic fabric

Kent State University Museum, Gift of Oscar de la Renta, 1986.33.33 a–b

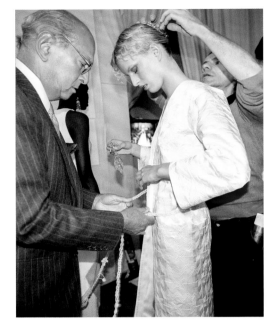

Dress (pl. 5), summer 1967
Yellow cotton and synthetic *matelassé*, metallic ribbon, bead appliqué
Kent State University Museum, Gift of Oscar de la Renta, 1986.33.4

Evening dress (pl. 2), fall 1967
Printed silk cloqué, Lurex, rhinestone appliqué
Fine Arts Museums of San Francisco, Gift of Constance B. Peabody, L15.36.1

Evening dress (pl. 6, variant), fall 1967
Black silk crepe
Rhode Island School of Design Museum, 2001.83.14

Cocktail dress (pl. 1), fall 1968
Black silk crepe, white satin, galloon edging, bead embellishment
Kent State University Museum, Gift of Oscar de la Renta, 1986.33.28 ab

Cocktail dress, ca. 1969
Printed silk, silk fringe
The Metropolitan Museum of Art, Gift of the Brooklyn Museum, 2009,
Gift of Mrs. Mike Epstein, 1971, 2009.300.7782

Jumpsuit (pl. 3), fall 1969
Printed silk organza
Fine Arts Museums of San Francisco, Gift of Doris Raymond, 1998.234.11a–b

Ensemble; coat and jumpsuit, fall 1969
Yellow plaid wool
The Metropolitan Museum of Art, Gift of Marion Poons, 1984, 1984.597.1a–e

Evening coat, fall 1969
Black leather, metal, fur trim
Private collection

Evening dress, fall 1969
Black silk velvet, bead and rhinestone embroidery
Private collection

Evening dress, spring 1974
Pale orange rayon knit
Cincinnati Art Museum, 1988.158

Evening dress (pl. 4), spring 1974
Azure-blue silk
FIDM Museum at the Fashion Institute of Design & Merchandising, Los Angeles;
Transfer from the Museum at the Fashion Institute of Technology, 97.291.18

Evening dress (fig. 23), spring 1974
Lime-green silk crepe de chine
Museum at the Fashion Institute of Technology, 86.130.68

SPAIN

Cocktail dress (pls. 19, 20), resort 1969
Printed silk organza
Kent State University Museum, Gift of Oscar de la Renta, 1986.33.16

Ensemble; tunic and pants, fall 1969
Red suede and silk chiffon, rhinestone and bead embellishment
Oscar de la Renta LLC, 5172

Evening dress (pl. 18), fall 1971
Black silk taffeta
Chicago History Museum, 1980.145.4abc

Dress (pl. 25), spring 1979
Black-and-white polka-dot print silk chiffon, white silk gazar
Collection of Pat Cleveland

Evening dress, ca. 1980
Black synthetic fabric
The Metropolitan Museum of Art, Gift of Mrs. Henry W. Breyer III, 1985, 1985.361.3

Evening ensemble; dress and bolero, ca. 1980s
Black silk, yellow silk, jet bead pom-poms
The Metropolitan Museum of Art, Gift of Nancy Reagan, 1995, 1995.71.1a, b

(previous spread)
69 Spring/summer 2002, Oscar de la Renta
for Pierre Balmain, January 2002

(this spread)
70 Spring/summer 2002, Oscar de la Renta
for Pierre Balmain, January 2002
71 Autumn/winter 2002–2003, Oscar
de la Renta for Pierre Balmain, July 2002
72 Autumn/winter 2002–2003, Oscar
de la Renta for Pierre Balmain, July 2002

Cocktail dress (pl. 24), fall 1986
Printed silk taffeta
Kent State University Museum, Gift of Lyn Revson, 1989.34.7

Evening ensemble; dress and bolero, 1988
Black-and-white polka-dot print silk satin, white silk crepe
The Metropolitan Museum of Art, Gift of Gail S. Davidson, 1996, 1996.490a–d

Evening dress, fall 1992
Ruby-red silk taffeta, burgundy silk velvet
FIDM Museum at the Fashion Institute of Design & Merchandising, Los Angeles; Gift of
Mrs. Clarissa Dyer, 2003.794.22

Oscar de la Renta for Pierre Balmain
Cape (pl. 13), autumn/winter 1993–1994
Saffron-yellow and fuchsia silk satin
Collection of Annette de la Renta

Evening dress (pl. 22), fall 1996
Sequin and bead embroidered black silk crepe
Collection of Annette de la Renta

Oscar de la Renta for Pierre Balmain
Evening coat (pl. 16), autumn/winter 1999–2000
Red double-faced cashmere and wool, silk faille, jet embroidery
Pierre Balmain

Oscar de la Renta for Pierre Balmain
Evening ensemble; blouse and skirt, autumn/winter 2000–2001
White silk tulle, black silk taffeta, bead embroidery
Fine Arts Museums of San Francisco, Gift of Mr. Thomas L. Kempner, 2007.34.76a–b
Worn by Nan Kempner

Oscar de la Renta for Pierre Balmain
Evening dress (pl. 23), autumn/winter 2000–2001
Black silk velvet, rhinestones
Private collection

Evening ensemble; dress and cape, 2001
Blue and yellow duchesse silk satin
Collection of Annette de la Renta

Custom evening ensemble; blouse and skirt (figs. 2–4), 2001
Navy silk taffeta, ruby-red silk taffeta, black silk satin
Oscar de la Renta LLC, 1434, 1428
Worn by Mica Ertegun

Oscar de la Renta for Pierre Balmain
Skirt (pl. 21), autumn/winter 2001–2002
Printed silk satin
Private collection

Oscar de la Renta for Pierre Balmain
Evening ensemble; dress and wrap, autumn/winter 2001–2002
Pink silk taffeta
Savannah College of Art and Design, SCAD Museum of Art,
Gift of Patricia Altschul, 2008.15.5A, B

Evening dress (pl. 17, variant), spring 2005
Black silk tulle, black silk taffeta appliqué
Collection of Annette de la Renta

Evening dress (pl. 15), resort 2010
Black silk faille, silk taffeta
Collection of Lynn Wyatt

Evening ensemble; dress and overblouse (fig. 34), spring 2012
Marigold silk taffeta, black floral-embroidered silk tulle
Oscar de la Renta LLC, 806

ASIA

Oscar de la Renta for Jane Derby
Dress (pl. 39, variant), resort 1967
Printed brocade, stone embellishment
Museum at the Fashion Institute of Technology, 79.147.5
Worn by Diana Vreeland

Caftan, fall 1967
Printed cotton and acetate brocade, stone embellishment
Museum at the Fashion Institute of Technology, 79.147.4
Worn by Diana Vreeland

Evening ensemble; tunic and pants (pl. 34), fall 1968
Jade-green wool, silk, Lurex, galloon banding
Oscar de la Renta LLC, 5171
Worn by Lynn Wyatt

Caftan, spring 1982
Hand-painted silk crepe de chine
Kent State University Museum, Silverman/Rodgers Collection, 1983.1.2058

Caftan (pl. 27), summer 1982
Hand-painted silk crepe de chine
Kent State University Museum, Silverman/Rodgers Collection, 1983.1.2057

Caftan, spring 1982
Hand-painted silk crepe de chine
Kent State University Museum, Silverman/Rodgers Collection, 1983.1.2059

Caftan, spring 1982
Hand-painted silk crepe de chine
Kent State University Museum, Silverman/Rodgers Collection, 1983.1.2060

Evening ensemble; tunic and pants (pl. 30), fall 1982
Printed silk, metallic lace, cording
FIDM Museum at the Fashion Institute of Design & Merchandising, Los Angeles;
Transfer from the Museum at the Fashion Institute of Technology, 97.291.17AB

Evening ensemble; jacket and pants (pl. 29), fall 1988
Black silk velvet, red bead embroidery, black silk
The Metropolitan Museum of Art, Anonymous Gift, 1993, 1993.137.8a–c

Oscar de la Renta for Pierre Balmain
Caftan (pl. 32), spring/summer 1997
Polychrome silk blend
The Metropolitan Museum of Art, Gift of Thomas L. Kempner, 2006, 2006.420.66
Worn by Nan Kempner

Evening ensemble; tunic and pants (pl. 37), fall 1997
Sapphire-blue silk velvet, silk chiffon, gold and green metallic hand-painted trim
Fine Arts Museums of San Francisco, Gift of Mr. Thomas L. Kempner, 2007.34.5a–b
Worn by Nan Kempner

Oscar de la Renta for Pierre Balmain
Evening ensemble; tunic and pants (pl. 38), autumn/winter 1999–2000
Red silk crepe de chine, black silk velvet, sable tails
The Metropolitan Museum of Art, Gift of Thomas L. Kempner, 2006, 2006.420.107a, b
Worn by Nan Kempner

Oscar de la Renta for Pierre Balmain
Evening ensemble; top and skirt (pl. 41), autumn/winter 1999–2000
Metallic brocaded silk
Pierre Balmain

Oscar de la Renta for Pierre Balmain
Evening ensemble; tunic and pants (pl. 40), autumn/winter 1999–2000
Black silk velvet, gold silk appliqué
Pierre Balmain

Oscar de la Renta for Pierre Balmain
Evening ensemble; coat and pants (pl. 33), spring/summer 2000
Polychrome silk taffeta, polychrome silk embroidery, turquoise silk shantung
Collection of Annette de la Renta

Oscar de la Renta for Pierre Balmain
Evening dress (pls. 35–36), autumn/winter 2002–2003
Embroidered silk, cornflower-blue silk taffeta
Collection of Ann Getty

Coat (pl. 31), spring 2005
Silk warp-resist dyeing (ikat)
Fine Arts Museums of San Francisco, Gift of Mr. Thomas L. Kempner, 2007.34.6a–b
Worn by Nan Kempner

Coat (pl. 28), fall 2013
Printed silk velvet, fox trim
Collection of Roberta Garza-Medina

RUSSIA

Evening dress (pls. 48–49), fall 1968
Polychrome lamé, sable, metallic braid
Phoenix Art Museum, 1987.C.23

Day ensemble; dress and coat (pl. 45, variant), fall 1970
Black wool with paisley trim, fox fur
Chicago History Museum, 1987.589.1ab

Evening ensemble; jacket, top, and skirt (pl. 44), fall 1981
Burgundy silk moiré faille, gold and bead appliqué, gold lace, burgundy plaid silk taffeta
Kent State University Museum, Gift of Aileen Mehle, 1987.87.60 a–d

Evening dress (pl. 47, variant), spring 1982
Raspberry silk gazar, bead embroidery
Kent State University Museum, Silverman/Rodgers Collection, 1983.1.2032

Ensemble; blouse and skirt (pl. 46), spring 1982
Orange and metallic striped silk chiffon, raspberry silk gauze
Kent State University Museum, Silverman/Rodgers Collection, 1983.1.2040 a–b

Evening ensemble; bodice and skirt (pl. 47, variant), spring 1982
Raspberry silk satin, bugle bead embroidery, emerald–green silk gauze
Kent State University Museum, Silverman/Rodgers Collection, 1983.1.2043 a–b

Evening ensemble; dress and over-bodice (pl. 42), fall 1984
Black silk velvet, gold lace, rhinestone embroidery
Kent State University Museum, Silverman/Rodgers Collection, 1983.1.1880 a–c

Custom wedding ensemble; jacket and skirt, 1985
Brown silk velvet, burgundy silk taffeta
Private collection

Evening ensemble; jacket and skirt (pl. 43), fall 1989
Printed silk, bead and sequin embroidery
Phoenix Art Museum, 2004.3.A–B

Oscar de la Renta for Pierre Balmain
Evening ensemble; dress and bolero, autumn/winter 1993–1994
Gold lamé, passementerie and rhinestone appliqué, black silk velvet
Pierre Balmain

Oscar de la Renta for Pierre Balmain
Evening coat (pl. 50), autumn/winter 1997–1998
Metallic stenciled olive-green silk velvet, sable
Pierre Balmain

Oscar de la Renta for Pierre Balmain
Evening ensemble; coat and pants (pl. 51), autumn/winter 1997–1998
Metallic stenciled silk velvet, sable, brown-striped silk taffeta
Pierre Balmain

Oscar de la Renta for Pierre Balmain
Evening dress (pl. 52), autumn/winter 1997–1998
Printed silk satin, sable trim
Pierre Balmain

Oscar de la Renta for Pierre Balmain
Evening dress (pl. 52), autumn/winter 1997–1998
Floral silk satin, sable trim
Private collection

Oscar de la Renta for Pierre Balmain
Coat, autumn/winter 1997–1998
Wool paisley, sable
Private collection

Oscar de la Renta for Pierre Balmain
Shawl, autumn/winter 1998–1999
Wool paisley, sable
Collection of Annette de la Renta

Oscar de la Renta for Pierre Balmain
Evening dress, autumn/winter 1998–1999
Silk taffeta, bead, sequin and metallic thread embroidery, chenille yarn
Texas Fashion Collection, University of North Texas,
College of Visual Arts and Design, 2009.001.014
Worn by Mercedes Bass

Oscar de la Renta for Pierre Balmain
Evening coat, autumn/winter 2000–2001
Patent leather and mink
Pierre Balmain

Oscar de la Renta for Pierre Balmain
Coat, autumn/winter 2002–2003
Embroidered and appliquéd burgundy wool, fur trim
Collection of Ann Getty

GARDEN

Evening ensemble; blouse and skirt, ca. 1978
Apple-green and gold silk taffeta
Museum at the Fashion Institute of Technology, 91.190.2
Worn by Penelope Tree

Evening ensemble; blouse and skirt (pl. 56), spring 1983
Printed silk organza, gray silk satin ribbon
Kent State University Museum, Gift of the Helen O. Borowitz Collection, 1993.81.12 a–c

Evening ensemble; blouse and skirt (pl. 56), spring 1983
Printed silk organza, pale-pink crepe, white silk satin ribbon
Kent State University Museum, Gift of Savanna M. Clark, 2001.49.1 a–d

Evening ensemble; blouse and skirt, ca. 1984–1986
Pink, rose, and olive silk taffeta
FIDM Museum at the Fashion Institute of Design & Merchandising, Los Angeles;
Gift of Mrs. Clarissa Dyer, 2003.794.13A–C

Oscar de la Renta for Pierre Balmain
Evening dress (pls. 63–64), spring/summer 1994
Green-and-white striped silk taffeta
Pierre Balmain

Oscar de la Renta for Pierre Balmain
Evening dress (pl. 66), spring/summer 1997
Pale-pink silk tulle
Pierre Balmain

Oscar de la Renta for Pierre Balmain
Evening ensemble; overdress and pants (pl. 59, variant), spring/summer 1998
Sky-blue and white-striped chiné silk taffeta
Collection of Annette de la Renta

Oscar de la Renta for Pierre Balmain
Cocktail dress (pl. 61), spring/summer 1998
Floral-printed silk taffeta
Pierre Balmain

Oscar de la Renta for Pierre Balmain
Cocktail dress (pl. 62), spring/summer 1998
Floral-printed silk taffeta
Pierre Balmain

Evening ensemble; overdress and skirt (pl. 55, variant), spring/summer 1999
Sky-blue and white-striped silk taffeta, gold silk taffeta
Collection of Ann Getty

Oscar de la Renta for Pierre Balmain
Evening ensemble; blouse and skirt (pl. 54), spring/summer 1999
Pink linen, pink silk taffeta
Pierre Balmain

Oscar de la Renta for Pierre Balmain
Evening ensemble; blouse, skirt, and shawl (pl. 57), spring/summer 2000
White silk organza, polychrome silk embroidery
Pierre Balmain

Oscar de la Renta for Pierre Balmain
Evening dress (pl. 65), autumn/winter 2000–2001
Embroidered jade-green silk, sable
Pierre Balmain

Oscar de la Renta for Pierre Balmain
Evening ensemble; bodice and skirt, autumn/winter 2001–2002
Printed silk taffeta
Private collection

Evening skirt, resort 2002
Printed silk taffeta
Collection of Alexandra Kotur

Custom evening dress (pl. 60), 2006
Blue-and-white chiné silk taffeta
Oscar de la Renta LLC, 5114
Worn by Kirsten Dunst

Evening dress (pl. 58), spring 2011
Green silk faille, pink and green silk embroidery and appliqué
Oscar de la Renta LLC, 703

Evening dress (pl. 58), spring 2011
Pink silk organza, eggshell cord embroidery, pink silk faille
Oscar de la Renta LLC

Evening dress (pl. 58), spring 2011
Black silk taffeta and *point d'esprit* lace
Private collection

Evening dress (pl. 58), spring 2011
Chartreuse silk faille
Private collection

Evening dress (pl. 58), spring 2011
Ivory silk faille, silk tulle, silk satin ribbon
Private collection

Evening dress (pl. 58), spring 2011
Pale-pink and gold silk organza, gold lamé
Private collection

Evening dress (pl. 58), spring 2011
Salmon-pink silk faille
Private collection

BALLROOM

Bridal gown, spring 1982
White silk gazar, gold cord embroidery
Kent State University Museum, Silverman/Rodgers Collection, 1983.001.2034

Oscar de la Renta for Pierre Balmain
Evening dress (pl. 85), autumn/winter 1996–1997
Black-and-white printed silk satin
Pierre Balmain

Oscar de la Renta for Pierre Balmain
Evening dress (pls. 69–70), autumn/winter 1999–2000
Black silk velvet, white silk embroidery and appliqué
Pierre Balmain

Oscar de la Renta for Pierre Balmain
Evening ensemble; jumpsuit and coat, autumn/winter 1999–2000
Pale-blue silk and silk taffeta, ostrich feathers
Pierre Balmain

Custom evening ensemble; dress and wrap (pl. 73), 2000
Printed chiné silk taffeta
Courtesy of Secretary Hillary Rodham Clinton

Evening ensemble; jacket and skirt (pl. 82), spring 2002
Silk tulle, bead and sequin embroidery
Mrs. Laura Bush and George W. Bush Presidential Library and Museum

Evening dress, fall 2003
Black silk tulle, black silk satin ribbon, bead and sequin embroidery, feathers
Fine Arts Museums of San Francisco, Gift of the family of Diana Dollar Knowles, L15.46.1

Oscar de la Renta for Pierre Balmain
Evening dress (pls. 74–75), autumn/winter 2002–2003
Silk, gold lamé, gilt cock feathers
Smithsonian National Museum of American History, 2003, 0274.002
Worn by Lee Radziwill

Evening dress, fall 2005
Gold silk net, sequin embroidery
Collection of Catie Marron

Evening dress (pl. 86, variant), fall 2005
Copper silk taffeta
Collection of Diane B. Wilsey

Evening dress (pl. 89), resort 2006
Green silk tulle, black lace, silk satin
Collection of Diane B. Wilsey

Evening dress (pl. 76), fall 2006
Burgundy silk velvet and silk satin
Private collection

Evening dress, 2011
Printed chiné silk taffeta
Private collection

Evening ensemble; jacket and skirt (pl. 84), pre-fall 2011
Gold lamé
Collection of Alexandra Kotur

Evening dress (pl. 88), resort 2012
White silk faille, red and green silk embroidery and appliqué
Oscar de la Renta LLC, 706
Worn by Rihanna

Evening dress, 2012
White silk organza, cotton lace, ostrich feathers, sequins
Private collection

Evening dress (pls. 77–78), pre-fall 2012
Pleated silver lamé
Oscar de la Renta LLC, 941
Worn by Jessica Chastain

Evening dress (pl. 68), fall 2012
Black silk, silk tulle
Oscar de la Renta LLC, 788
Worn by Penélope Cruz

(this spread)
82 Spring/summer 2002, Oscar de la Renta for Pierre Balmain, January 2002
83 Spring 2004, Oscar de la Renta, September 2003
84 Spring 2004, Oscar de la Renta, September 2003

(following spread)
85 Autumn/winter 2002–2003, Oscar de la Renta for Pierre Balmain, January 2002
86 Spring 2004, Oscar de la Renta, September 2003
87 Autumn/winter 2002–2003, Oscar de la Renta for Pierre Balmain, July 2002
88 Spring/summer 2002, Oscar de la Renta for Pierre Balmain, January 2002

Evening dress (pl. 67, variants) fall 2012
Black and gray silk tulle
Oscar de la Renta LLC, 1319

Evening dress (pl. 87), spring 2012
Emerald-green silk taffeta, black Battenberg lace
Oscar de la Renta LLC, 829
Worn by Nicki Minaj

Custom evening dress (pl. 79), 2013
Pale-blue silk tulle
Private collection

Evening dress (pls. 71–72), fall 2013
Violet silk faille, metallic embroidery
Oscar de la Renta LLC, 1239

Evening dress (pl. 72), fall 2013
Fuchsia silk faille, metallic embroidery
Oscar de la Renta LLC, 1308

Custom evening dress (pl. 81), 2014
Pink silk organza, silk and bead embroidery
Private collection

Custom evening dress (pl. 80), 2014
White duchesse satin, black silk velvet
Private collection

Evening dress, fall 2014
Black silk satin, gold lamé, gilt feather appliqué
Oscar de la Renta LLC, 1515
Worn by Karlie Kloss

Evening dress (pl. 83), pre-fall 2014
Brown, gold, and pink silk taffeta
Oscar de la Renta LLC, 1457

Evening dress (pl. 83), pre-fall 2014
Pink, purple, and green silk taffeta
Oscar de la Renta LLC, 1463

Evening dress (pl. 83), resort 2015
Purple silk faille
Oscar de la Renta LLC, 1569

Selected Bibliography

BOOKS

Blass, Bill, and Cathy Horyn. *Bare Blass*. New York: HarperCollins, 2002.

Bowles, Hamish. *Balenciaga and Spain*. San Francisco: Fine Arts Museums of San Francisco, 2011.

Demarchelier, Patrick. *Patrick Demarchelier*. Göttingen, Germany: steidlDangin, 2008.

Devlin, Polly. *Vogue Book of Fashion Photography, 1919–1979*. New York: Simon and Schuster, 1979.

Druesedow, Jean L., and Eric Burns. *Oscar de la Renta: American Elegance*. Kent, Ohio: Kent State University Museum, 2006.

Elgort, Arthur. *Arthur Elgort's Models Manual*. Göttingen, Germany: Steidl, 2014.

Friedan, Betty. *The Feminine Mystique*. New York: W. W. Norton, 2013.

Givhan, Robin. *The Battle of Versailles*. New York: Flatiron Books, 2015.

Gray, Francine du Plessix. *Them: A Memoir of Parents*. New York: Penguin, 2005.

Hall-Duncan, Nancy. *The History of Fashion Photography*. New York: Alpine, 1979.

Harrison, Martin. *Appearances: Fashion Photography Since 1945*. New York: Rizzoli, 1991.

Kazanjian, Dodie, and Calvin Tomkins. *Alex: The Life of Alexander Liberman*. New York: Alfred A. Knopf, 1993.

Lewis, Alfred Allan, and Constance Woodworth. *Miss Elizabeth Arden: An Unretouched Portrait*. New York: Coward, McCann & Geoghegan, 1972.

Mackenzie Stuart, Amanda. *Empress of Fashion: A Life of Diana Vreeland*. New York: HarperCollins, 2012.

Mallis, Fern. *Fashion Lives: Fashion Icons with Fern Mallis*. New York: Rizzoli, 2015.

Milbank, Caroline Rennolds. *Couture: The Great Designers*. New York: Stewart, Tabori & Chang, 1985.

Mirabella, Grace. *In and Out of Vogue*. New York: Doubleday, 1995.

Mower, Sarah. *Oscar: The Style, Inspiration and Life of Oscar de la Renta*. New York: Assouline, 2002.

Purcell, Kerry William. *Alexey Brodovitch*. New York: Phaidon, 2002.

Rydell, Robert W. *World of Fairs: The Century-of-Progress Expositions*. Chicago: University of Chicago Press, 1993.

Sorkin, Molly, and Jennifer Park, eds. *Joaquín Sorolla and the Glory of Spanish Dress*. New York: Queen Sofía Spanish Institute, 2011.

Vreeland, Alexander, ed. *Memos: The Vogue Years, 1962–1971*. New York: Rizzoli, 2013.

Vreeland, Diana. *D.V.* New York: Da Capo, 1984.

Walz, Barbra, and Bernadine Morris. *The Fashion Makers*. New York: Random House, 1978.

Wilcox, Claire. *The Golden Age of Couture: Paris and London, 1947–1957*. London: V & A, 2007.

PERIODICALS

"Arden Shows Designs by de la Renta." *New York Times*, September 19, 1963.

Bender, Marilyn. "Coty Awards Are Voted to George Halley and Luba of Elite." *New York Times*, June 21, 1968.

Bernstein, Jacob. "Helmut Newton: Lensman Provocateur." *Women's Wear Daily*, January 26, 2004, 16.

Bowles, Hamish. "The Room with a View." *Vogue*, December 2008, 318.

Brantley, Ben. "Slim and Simple, New York 1982." *Women's Wear Daily*, September 30, 1981, 30.

Chang, Samantha V. "Asia Major." *Vogue*, December 2010, 299.

"De la Renta's Best Seller." *Women's Wear Daily*, May 14, 1970, 1.

"De la Renta's 7th Avenue Debut Is a Hit." *New York Times*, June 11, 1965.

Donovan, Carrie. "Diana Vreeland, Dynamic Fashion Figure, Joins *Vogue*: Editor Created Fashion Image in Former Job." *New York Times*, March 28, 1962.

Doyle, Kevin, and Godfrey Deeny. "Oscar Sews Up Couture, RTW Deal at Balmain." *Women's Wear Daily*, November 17, 1992, 24.

Emerson, Gloria. "Feminine Enchantment Is Captured in Paris Adaptations." *New York Times*, March 8, 1960.

"The Eye." *Women's Wear Daily*, April 13, 1964, 1.

"The Eye." *Women's Wear Daily*, February 21, 1962, 1.

"The Eye." *Women's Wear Daily*, January 9, 1963, 1.

"The Eye." *Women's Wear Daily*, January 10, 1963, 6.

Fallon, James. "Anna Wintour Takes Charge." *Women's Wear Daily*, November 5, 1986.

"The Fashion Chief." *Women's Wear Daily*, November 30, 1962.

Feitelberg, Rosemary. "Lucky Lindy." *Women's Wear Daily*, March 27, 2015.

Friedman, Arthur. "Oscar, Balmain Talking about a Couture Line." *Women's Wear Daily*, October 6, 1992, 1.

Friedman, Vanessa. "As Old (and New) as Time: Michael Kors, Oscar de la Renta and More." *New York Times*, September 10, 2014.

Gross, Michael. "War of the Poses: *Bazaar*'s New Liz Takes on *Vogue*'s Anna." *New York Magazine*, April 27, 1992.

Haynes, Kevin. "Anna Wintour." *Women's Wear Daily*, September 1989.

"High Chic-a-boom." *Women's Wear Daily*, August 25, 1978, 1.

Hochswender, Woody. "Changes at *Vogue*: A Complex Tale of Rumors and Facts." *New York Times*, July 25, 1988.

Horyn, Cathy. "Fashion Review; In Paris, Discipline, Decadence, and the Old Order Changes." *New York Times*, July 14, 2002.

Horyn, Cathy, and Enid Nemy. "Oscar de la Renta, Who Clothed Stars and Became One, Dies at 82." *New York Times*, October 20, 2014.

Iredale, Jessica. "Fashion Photographer Deborah Turbeville." *Women's Wear Daily*, October 28, 2013.

"Jane Derby Dead; Fashion Designer." *New York Times*, August 9, 1965.

Jefferson, Margo. "The Art and Business of Courting the Camera: *Arthur Elgort's Models Manual*." *New York Times*, July 6, 1994.

Kazanjian, Dodie. "Alexander Liberman (1912–1999)." *Vogue*, January 2000, 30.

Lichtenstein, Grace. "Feminists Demand 'Liberation' in *Ladies' Home Journal* Sit-In." *New York Times*, March 19, 1970.

"Longuette for Fall: Oscar de la Renta." *Women's Wear Daily*, May 8, 1970, 5.

"Master Designs for the Town and Country Woman." *Town and Country*, September 1968, 122.

Mazzaraco, Margaret. "Art by the Yard." *Women's Wear Daily*, February 18, 1981, 37.

McKinley, Jesse. "Helmut Newton Is Dead at 83." *New York Times*, January 25, 2004.

Menkes, Suzy. "Mario Testino at 30 Years." *New York Times*, October 2, 2011.

Morris, Bernadine. "Arden Styles Balance Austerity and Extravagance." *New York Times*, March 5, 1964.

——. "Arden Fashions Are Sleek by Day, Lavish at Night." *New York Times*, February 18, 1965.

——. "Fashions That Take the Focus Off the Hemline." *New York Times*, May 8, 1970.

——. "The Idea Is Not To Be Kooky, and Not To Be Boring, Either." *New York Times*, October 31, 1973.

——. "Review/Fashion; Playing It Safe in Paris." *New York Times*, October 24, 1991.

——. "Taffeta and Lace: Return of an Old, Romantic Look." *New York Times*, November 4, 1969, 48.

Nemy, Enid. "Henry Clarke, 77, Photographer of High Fashion for Magazines." *New York Times*, May 5, 1996.

Newton, Helmut. "The Eyes of Helmut Newton." *New York Magazine*, December 4, 1978.

"New Winner Chalked Up by de la Renta." *Women's Wear Daily*, May 15, 1970, 37.

"Oscar's Boom-Boom Dress." *Women's Wear Daily*, October 22, 1991, 1.

Reed, Julia. "Couture Conquistador: Where Worlds Collide." *Vogue*, March 2004, 740.

"Renta's Night Flights." *Women's Wear Daily*, November 17, 1978, 1.

Sheppard, Eugenia. "Inside Fashion: Oscar's Arabian Nights." *Women's Wear Daily*, June 6, 1968, 10.

——. "What's Ahead in Fall Fashion." *Des Moines (IA) Register*, June 13, 1967.

Sones, Melissa. "Oscar Goes Global." *Mirabella*, April 1991, 151.

Socha, Miles. "De la Renta to Exit Balmain." *Women's Wear Daily*, July 8, 2002, 2.

Spindler, Amy M. "Fashion Review; Marking Time for the Millennium." *New York Times*, July 28, 1998.

Taylor, Angela. "Coty's Winnie Given to Oscar." *New York Times*, June 30, 1967.

——. "The Deborah Turbeville Look: Altering the Focus on Fashion." *New York Times*, January 24, 1977.

Thompson, Hunter S. "The 'Hashbury' Is the Capital of the Hippies." *New York Times*, May 14, 1967.

"Two New Fashionables to New York." *Women's Wear Daily*, February 25, 1963, 5.

"Versailles." *Women's Wear Daily*, October 16, 1973, 1.

Women's Wear Daily, January 11, 1963, 1.

Women's Wear Daily, May 7, 1969, 1.

Women's Wear Daily, October 2, 1963, 30.

Women's Wear Daily, October 21, 1992, 8.

OTHER SOURCES

Cottam, Daniel Milford. "Paquin: Parisian Fashion Designs 1897–1954." *Victoria and Albert Museum* (blog). http://www.vam.ac.uk/blog/factory-presents/paquin-parisian-fashion-designs-1897-1954.

Coty American Fashion Critics' Awards 1967. "Coty Awards 1967 Programs and Winners." Eleanor Lambert Records, Special Collections and College Archives, Gladys Marcus Library, Fashion Institute of Technology-SUNY.

Oscar. 1972. Hearst Metrotone News, United States Information Agency.

"Oscar de la Renta Spring 2009" (includes an interview with Linda Fargo). YouTube video, 4:04. Posted by Bergdorf Goodman, January 9, 2009. https://www.youtube.com/watch?v=IQG07ShFpg0.

Phelps, Nicole. "Spring 2015 Ready-to-Wear, Oscar de la Renta." Style.com. Posted September 9, 2014. http://www.style.com/fashion-shows/spring-2015-ready-to-wear/oscar-de-la-renta.

"Pierre Balmain Haute Couture Spring 1993" (includes an interview with Elsa Klensch for CNN Style). YouTube video, 2:25. Posted February 7, 2015. https://www.youtube.com/watch?v=dt3FW5TaNlE.

"Treasures of American History: Creative Masterpieces, Minerva Dress by Oscar de la Renta." National Museum of American History. http://americanhistory.si.edu/treasures/creative-masterpieces.

Index

Note: Page numbers in italics refer to illustrations. Captions are indexed as text.

Photography Credits

Backstage at the 2013
spring collection, 2012

Published by the Fine Arts Museums of San Francisco and DelMonico Books • Prestel on the occasion of the exhibition *Oscar de la Renta*, de Young, San Francisco, March 12–May 30, 2016

This exhibition is organized by the Fine Arts Museums of San Francisco with the collaboration of Oscar de la Renta LLC.

PRESENTING SPONSORS
Cynthia Fry Gunn and John A. Gunn

DIRECTOR'S CIRCLE
Diane B. Wilsey

CURATOR'S CIRCLE
The Diana Dollar Knowles Foundation
Marissa Mayer and Zachary Bogue

BENEFACTOR'S CIRCLE
Paula and Bandel Carano
Stephanie and Jim Marver
Neiman Marcus

PATRON'S CIRCLE
Mrs. Carole McNeil
Mr. and Mrs. Joseph O. Tobin II

The catalogue is published with the assistance of the Andrew W. Mellon Foundation Endowment for Publications.

Library of Congress Cataloging-in-Publication Data

Oscar de la Renta (Fine Arts Museums of San Francisco)
  Oscar de la Renta / André Leon Talley, Molly Sorkin, Jennifer Park.
      pages cm
  "Published by the Fine Arts Museums of San Francisco and DelMonico Books / Prestel on the occasion of the exhibition Oscar de la Renta."
  Includes bibliographical references and index.
  ISBN 978-3-7913-5523-8 (trade) — ISBN 978-3-7913-6662-3 (pbk.) — ISBN 978-3-7913-6661-6 (museum) 1. De la Renta, Oscar—Exhibitions. 2. Fashion designers—United States—Exhibitions. 3. Costume design—United States—History—20th century—Exhibitions. 4. Costume design—United States—History—21st century—Exhibitions. 5. Fashion design—United States—History—20th century—Exhibitions. 6. Fashion design—United States—History—21st century—Exhibitions. I. Talley, André Leon. II. Sorkin, Molly. III. Park, Jennifer. IV. De la Renta, Oscar. Works. Selections. V. Fine Arts Museums of San Francisco, organizer, host institution. VI. Title.
  TT505.D4O54 2016
  746.9'2—dc23

Fine Arts Museums of San Francisco
Golden Gate Park
50 Hagiwara Tea Garden Drive
San Francisco, CA 94118–5402
www.famsf.org

Leslie Dutcher, Director of Publications
Jane Hyun, Editor
Danica Michels Hodge, Editor
Diana K. Murphy, Editorial Assistant

Edited by Kathryn Shedrick
Proofread by Susan Richmond
Picture research by Diana K. Murphy and Jenny Moussa Spring
Index by Nancy Wolff
Designed and typeset by Bob Aufuldish, Aufuldish & Warinner
Production management by Karen Farquhar
Separations, printing, and binding by Conti Tipocolor, Italy

DelMonico Books, an imprint of Prestel, a member of Verlagsgruppe Random House GmbH

Prestel Verlag
Neumarkter Strasse 28
81673 Munich
Tel.: +49 89 4136 0
Fax: +49 89 4136 2335

Prestel Publishing Ltd.
14-17 Wells Street
London W1T 3PD
Tel.: +44 20 7323 5004
Fax: +44 20 7323 0271

Prestel Publishing
900 Broadway, Suite 603
New York, NY 10003
Tel.: +1 212 995 2720
Fax: +1 212 995 2733
Email: sales@prestel-usa.com
www.prestel.com

978-3-7913-5523-8 (trade hardcover)
978-3-7913-6661-6 (museum hardcover)
978-3-7913-6662-3 (paperback)
978-3-7913-6677-7 (special hardcover)